HEARTS
KNIT
TOGETHER

TALKS FROM THE 1995
WOMEN'S CONFERENCE

Other volumes in the Women's Conference Series:

HEARTS
KNIT
TOGETHER

TALKS FROM THE 1995 WOMEN'S CONFERENCE

EDITED BY
SUSETTE FLETCHER GREEN
DAWN HALL ANDERSON
DLORA HALL DALTON

DESERET BOOK COMPANY
SALT LAKE CITY, UTAH

© 1996 Deseret Book Company

Library of Congress Catalog Card Number 96-84032

ISBN 1-57345-153-3

Printed in the United States of America

10   9   8   7   6   5   4   3   2   1

CONTENTS

CONTENTS

LIFE AFTER FIFTY

REJOICING IN EACH OTHER'S GIFTS

IN SEARCH OF SPIRIT

WOMEN'S BODIES, WOMEN'S SOULS

PREFACE

This book is the tenth in a series from the annual Women's Conference sponsored jointly by Brigham Young University and the Relief Society of The Church of Jesus Christ of Latter-day Saints. The essays and poems in this volume were drawn from presentations given at the 1995 conference.

We thank all those who made this volume possible. Jeanne Inouye chaired the conference and with her able committee of BYU faculty members and the Relief Society representatives spent many hours planning and coordinating the sessions. Suzanne Brady of Deseret Book has offered superb support, advice, and assistance in turning the manuscript into a book.

Very few of our authors are professional writers, and we particularly thank them for risking to tell their stories and to share their successes and failures, their insights and expertise with the larger community of Latter-day Saint women.

HEARTS KNIT TOGETHER

SANDRA ROGERS

One afternoon in the San Francisco library, while leafing through a thick volume of journals, I came upon an article on Mormonism. The author, a sociologist, was interested in how an American-born church became a worldwide religion. How, he questioned, would Mormonism shift from being a religion for the homogeneous to being a religion for the diverse?[1]

Managing worldwide diversity is a challenge for the Church. But, in truth, no matter where they live, be it the Wasatch Front or West Africa, today's Saints already come in many varieties. We differ in size, education, ethnicity, political preference, and accent. We differ in the clothes we choose, how much money we have, how much money we want, how well we cook, what we like to eat, the kind of work we do in or out of the home, our marital and family situations. The length of time we have been in the Church may be different. So are our sufferings—whether we are mothers or just wishing we could be—the things that are hard for us to do, the things that hurt us, the things that give us joy, the mistakes we have made, the successes we have enjoyed.

Yet with all this variation, "all are alike unto God" (2 Nephi 26:33). Becoming sensitive to each other—allowing for and respecting differences—helps us all feel welcome, wanted, and

Sandra Rogers is dean of the College of Nursing at Brigham Young University. She was a Welfare Services missionary in the Philippines and now serves in her ward Relief Society.

needed in the Church. But that is not the only reason our hearts must be knit together. The most compelling and urgent reason is that without unity we simply cannot be Christ's. If we cannot attain unity, we are disobedient to him, for the Lord has said, "Be one; and if ye are not one ye are not mine" (D&C 38:27).

In the Book of Mormon, Alma taught new Church members that "there should be no contention one with another, but . . . they should look forward with one eye, having one faith and one baptism, having their hearts knit together in unity and in love one towards another" (Mosiah 18:21). Without this unifying love, we are as sounding brass and tinkling cymbals—nice for a small round-the-block parade but unsuitable for a resounding heavenly choir. "Hearts knit together in unity and love" means much more than sharing warm feelings on Sunday, caring about your neighbors, or even being loyal friends. Alma is describing how to be covenant keepers, for all the law and the prophets depend on loving God with all our heart, might, mind, and strength and our neighbors as ourselves (see Matthew 22:37–40). To be without contention, we must also knit our hearts to Christ, the author of the "everlasting covenant, even the fulness of [his] gospel" (D&C 66:2). In this way, our hearts are knit together not merely with our own unity and love but with his.

Our love must be grounded in his because, as Paul taught, "And though I bestow all my goods to feed the poor, and though I give my body to be burned, and have not charity, it profiteth me nothing" (1 Corinthians 13:3). Why would Paul say bestowing all our goods to feed the poor isn't the same as charity? I see faithful members of my ward canning peaches at the welfare cannery, or rising at 4 A.M. to work in the temple laundry, or taking a neighbor's children for an afternoon. I see meals prepared for the sick, the grieving, or those bowed down—meals that if lined up dish to dish would circle the globe twice over and keep Deseret Industries supplied for years with orphaned pans and bowls. How can Paul tell me that might not be "never-failing charity"?

Is there some holier form of compassion than service? What sanctifies our service?

I have come to believe that to knit our hearts in Christ's perfect unity and love we must first "break" our hearts. We must be humble. The scriptures and our leaders repeatedly affirm that humility is the prerequisite for faith, hope, and charity. Mormon, for instance, tells us that we "cannot have faith and hope, save [we] shall be meek, and lowly of heart. . . . For none is acceptable before God, save the meek and lowly in heart" (Moroni 7:43–44). President Ezra Taft Benson taught that the test of the twentieth-century Church is pride.[2] Pride is for us as the frozen snow of Wyoming was for the Willie and Martin handcart companies. Pride keeps us from humility, and without humility we cannot have charity and unity.

Paul makes more sense considered in that light: the prideful bestowal of all our goods to feed the poor can never be charity. Humility perfects our unity and purifies our love. Without humility, our fondness for and loyalty to each other can, in some circumstances, lead us away from the light of Christ, not closer to it. Without humility, our unity can become self-serving, restrictive, and haughty, directing us straight up the steps of a latter-day rameumptom instead of into the sandaled, dusty footprints of the Master. Satan's counterfeit for hearts being knit together in unity and love is not contentious or apathetic hearts; it is proud hearts seeking other proud hearts in self-congratulation.

King Benjamin taught that humility begins when we acknowledge our dependence upon God our Father and the Savior, Jesus Christ, for life and breath here and for eternal joy in the hereafter. Humility is knowing that because of the Atonement, we can, if we "yield to the enticings of the Holy Spirit" and follow Christ, be saved from sin, as well as from carelessness, inadequacy, bitterness, anger, revenge, poor esteem, selfishness, fear, and all the other tendencies of the natural woman (see Mosiah 3:19). Whatever brings us to the well, the vessel into which his healing, comforting Spirit is poured is the broken heart.

The Savior has often begged us to come unto him. He pleads, "Come unto me, all ye that labour and are heavy laden, and I will give you rest. Take my yoke upon you, and learn of me; for I am meek and lowly in heart: and ye shall find rest unto your souls" (Matthew 11:28–29). To Joseph Smith he said, "Learn of me, and listen to my words; walk in the meekness of my Spirit, and you shall have peace in me" (D&C 19:23). Humility, walking in meekness, is the prerequisite condition of the heart.

I would like to share one woman's humility with you. My grandmother Malinda Porter Rogers was born in a little town in northern Arizona. Her father farmed and was the mail carrier. Grandma struggled in school and completed only the eighth grade. Seven years after she married, her father was tragically killed in an accident with a mail train. Then in 1936, her oldest sons, ages twelve and nine, drowned in a whirlpool created by the railroad siphoning water from the river. Four years later, her husband—my grandfather—died of a kidney ailment. Many of his friends said he died of grief over the loss of his boys. Grandma faced life with five children and no savings, no previous work experience, no food stamps, no government relief, and no lawsuit against the railroad.

The elders quorum repaired a small, one-bedroom home for the family. Her widowed mother came to live with her, and Grandma eventually buried her mother in the dress Grandma had worn for her eighth-grade graduation and again for her wedding. She came close to losing her home several years later when her brother convinced her to mortgage it to lend him money and then "forgot" to make the payments.

She washed the bishop's milking equipment at his dairy in exchange for milk for the family. She cleaned the church, kneeling to scrub the crayon marks off the linoleum of the nursery, in return for Church assistance. She turned collars on shirts. She could mend a corner tear in the sheerest of fabric with stitches invisible to the eye. If she ever went out for dinner, she invariably picked the least expensive item on the menu.

When her last child married, she gave her own little house to the newlyweds and never owned her own home again. She was a faithful visiting teacher and contributed her widow's mite to build the Relief Society Building in Salt Lake City. And never once did anyone hear her express doubt, self-pity, bitterness, depression, or anger. Never.

I don't think she was ever treated as Job was treated, being asked what terrible sins she had committed to deserve what had happened to her, but she was asked on several occasions how she kept going. Her answer, in perfect patience and meekness, not murmuring about her pressing, lifelong poverty, was, "I rely on the Lord, and he has blessed me."

Grandma was humble before she lost her sons and her husband. But her humility and faith refined her until she was the epitome of charity. For Grandma suffered long, was kind, envied not, was not puffed up, sought not her own, was not easily provoked, thought no evil, rejoiced in truth, bore all things, believed all things, hoped all things, and endured all things, and I know it shall be well with her at the last day (see Moroni 7:45, 47; 1 Corinthians 13:4–7).

This granddaughter needs to learn much to be equal to her grandmother. As I begin in tentative ways to understand humility—backing away from judgment, opening my heart, peeling off a bit of pride—my weaknesses loom before me with heightened clarity. That's not always comfortable; in fact, sometimes it's quite painful. But the Lord has promised to help turn those weaknesses into strengths if we come unto him, and I find myself holding on to that promise with great hope (see Ether 12:27). As I have tried to be more patient, more teachable, more forgiving, and more understanding of another's circumstances, I have felt more peace.

I grew up in a small town where everyone knew everyone else. After my mission, every time I went home to visit it seemed someone would ask, "Sandra, haven't you been able to catch a husband yet?" Not understanding much about the doctrine of humble hearts knit together in unity and love, I dreaded the questions, sometimes feeling that people were picking at a weakness, a void in my character. One day, speeding across the reservation between Page and Flagstaff, Arizona, I dreaded coming face to face with many at home who would remind me of my singleness—again.

Then a beam of pure light entered my heart through a tiny crack. I remembered my feelings for the men and women who always asked me those infernal questions. I remembered how they had taught me in Primary or Mutual or Sunday School. I remembered their goodness as neighbors. The Spirit whispered through the tiny crack in my heart, "My land, Sandra, get a grip." (The Spirit always speaks in language you understand.) "These people care about you. They are interested in you. They have no idea what kind of job you have so they can't ask about it. Their questions come out of their neighborliness and their interest—not because they want to hurt you. Be grateful." The questions came when I arrived home, but I felt no resentment, no sense of inadequacy. I stopped judging their intent as hurtful and started viewing it, instead, as love and concern.

Lessons of humility are often learned in a rigorous school. And I find that I must keep paying my tuition. Sometimes we are compelled to be humble because our God-given resources are inadequate to the challenges we face. Sometimes social or economic conditions compel us to humility, as with the poor Zoramites cast out of their synagogues because of their exceeding poverty. And sometimes we cultivate humility. As Alma taught, "Blessed are they who humble themselves without being compelled to be humble" (Alma 32:16).

Perhaps genuine humility is recognizing the source of true strength. The poor in spirit who come unto Christ and rely on his strength display a special brand of courage. They are willing to give up self-seeking and selfish concerns to know God. To be humble, we must be willing, as Alma says, to experience "a change of heart . . . [to be] stripped of pride . . . [and] of envy" (Alma 5:26, 28–29). Not only must we stop "tak[ing] advantage" of each other "because of [our] words" and "dig[ging] a pit for [our] neighbor[s]" (2 Nephi 28:8) but we must seek to bless the lives of others. Humility will help us magnify our callings; it will also teach us how to uphold "by [our] confidence, faith, and prayer" others who are fulfilling callings that are not ours (D&C 107:22).

Humility and charity help us serve without making unrighteous judgments. We do not need to know how or why the person we are serving got into that situation in the first place. We may trust that "what God hath cleansed, that call thou not common" (Acts 10:15). The greatest form of charity may be to withhold judgment.

Lisa Flindt, a senior graduating in nursing from Brigham Young University, wrote in her nursing journal of an experience that first broke and then opened her heart to feelings of unity and love: "Taking care of AIDS patients has made me take a hard look at my values. Though I have always felt the individual to be of infinite worth to our Father in Heaven, I have never before associated with people who were experiencing trials so different from mine and who needed Heavenly Father's infinite love so much. I learned the deeper meaning of charity when I cared for a wheelchair-bound HIV patient. He had lesions on his hands and buttocks, was pale as a ghost with a splotchy red rash consuming his body, and wore dark sunglasses which made him seem even ghastlier. His partner sat at his bedside. Initially, looking at the men made me feel physically ill. I wanted to hold my breath, toss the patient his gown, and spend as little time in the room as possible for I feared that inevitably he would sneeze, somehow I would catch his disease and then bring it home to my husband and ten-month-old baby.

"However, one day his mother entered the room. When she went to him, kissed him on the forehead, and whispered, 'Sweetheart, I will never leave you,' the words *charity never faileth* came to mind and my soul melted. I put on my gloves, picked up a bottle of lotion at his bedside and asked him if he wanted a back rub. That day I felt I understood the words of the Savior as never before, 'If ye have done it unto the least of these my brethren, ye have done it unto me.'

"Christ is the ultimate healer, and as nurses we are learning many aspects of the healer's art. Sometimes in the process of healing another's wounds, we must cross the barriers defining our own value system and dig deep into the heart of a suffering individual who may have values different from our own.

"I have been raised with the belief that homosexuality and IV-drug abuse are immoral, unethical, and simply wrong. Though I do not sacrifice my moral and ethical standards for the sake of tolerance, a turning point came in my life when I had to decide whether I would love others for who they are, surrendering judgment and criticism, or allow prejudgments and the social barriers of the world to stifle another's spiritual growth, as well as my own."[3]

Not long ago I had a short conversation with my bishop. I expressed sorrow and regret for something I had said, and my good bishop's response was, "That's all right, Sister Rogers. I know your heart is in the right place." Imagine how well we could serve, teach, encourage, uplift, and comfort one another, and how less frequently we would judge, feel judged, hurt, or left out and strike back at others if we stopped ascribing sinister or unkind motives to others and remembered their hearts are probably in the right place.

Hearts knit together rarely trouble each other with the "should" list but rather reason together about priorities. Hearts knit together in unity and love stop thinking that the measure of our homemaking efforts is the number of bodies in the seats and notice instead if and when the hearts that *are* there are being uplifted and strengthened. Hearts knit together in unity and love are offended less often, recover more quickly from hurt, and serve with less fanfare and more courage.

Some of my greatest challenges in humble charity have come in my reactions to people who should "know better" or from whom I have "expected better." My youngest brother made choices that took him away from the Church. He hurt my parents deeply, and I was angry—especially because he "knew better." I found tension in every interaction with this charming, personable, hard-working brother of mine. Several years after his abrupt departure from the Church, I had one of those all-too-brief moments of enlightenment when my hard heart broke just a little. (Humble hearts are teachable hearts—and I confess the Spirit has had to work to reach me sometimes.) The Spirit communicated, "Sandra, you spent hours on your mission teaching people who had been involved in almost every kind of sin and bad choice imaginable. Yet you loved them, and you testified to them that Christ loved them and that through the Atonement they could be reconciled to God. You accepted them with patience, and you treated them with kindness. Can't you do the same for your younger brother?" I have since felt peace in loving my brother and others who were taught to share my faith but who have made choices different from my own.

Hearts knit together in oneness and charity celebrate all that is good in each other. Humble hearts surround their expectations of another with a cocoon of gentleness and charity. Hearts knit in unity and love are not envious or demeaning of another's gifts. They are not jealous of another's material blessings. They know that God's promised blessings are rarely listed as assets on the world's balance sheet.

I had been involved in graduate research work in Nigeria

9

for several months when my Relief Society president, Faustina Otoo, invited me to her home for dinner. She seemed a bit apprehensive and apologized for the circumstances in which she lived as if she were inviting some royal personage who had never eaten a meal anywhere but the Waldorf-Astoria. I learned later that she had attended a Relief Society lesson on being "no more strangers or foreigners" that had helped her see that I was a stranger in her part of the world, and the Lord wanted her to help me feel welcome, even though she feared I would be uncomfortable in her home or look down on her. Determined to do what the Lord wanted, she humbled herself and exposed her extreme poverty to me.

To make me as comfortable as possible, she arranged with her landlady for me to use the landlord's private bathroom so I wouldn't be faced with the community facility, which was somewhat austerely appointed. I would be staying overnight, and she felt panicky because I would have to sleep on the floor. American television had taught her that I would be expecting to sleep in my own, private, king-sized bed.

That evening she proudly showed me her growing collection of Church literature, reaffirming her testimony of the gospel of Jesus Christ. I did everything I could to show her I was comfortable in her home—because I was—and Faustina and I became dear friends. The entire friendship began because of her humility.

Now, listen to the same story from her perspective.

"Sandra . . . was living in Lagos to do her doctorate work. She took an interest in me. . . . I was down and very sad. She said she wanted to comfort me, but I wouldn't give her the chance. I never wanted to invite her to my house, because I have always had the impression that whites live in a unique environment, and where I live is not good enough to invite a missionary or white person to. So I never invited anybody.

"We were having a lesson in Relief Society that said that we in the gospel are 'no more strangers . . . but fellowcitizens'

(Ephesians 2:19). I told Sandra that I had always really wanted to invite her to my place. She said she didn't mind how I lived, so I invited her.

"She humbled herself to the extent that she slept on the floor with me. . . . We read the scriptures together, and that was the first time I had had that type of experience. . . . I told Sandra that she has showed me the life I think Christ wanted his children to have. . . . I will send her my birth certificate and other papers, so that should I happen to die, she can go to the temple and do my temple work for me.

"She lowered herself to befriend *me*—somebody who doesn't have any background. I am nothing that she should become my friend."[4]

Dear Faustina is poor in the things of the world and rich in the things of God. If humility could knit the heart of Faustina (a short, poor, married-and-then-divorced mother, former Pentecostal, uneducated but self-taught black woman who works as a seamstress) with the heart of Sandi (a tall, not-so-economically-challenged, born-in-the-Church, educationally privileged, single, white woman who teaches at a university), then I believe humble, broken hearts can bring any and all of us together in unity and love.

Do you find on occasion, as I do, a discouraging gap between righteous desires so deeply felt on Sunday and the realities of living on Monday? Humility is hardest to have when we need it the most. But we can cultivate humility even when we struggle with pride, when we feel attacked, when we feel misunderstood, when we are afraid, when we doubt, when we feel perfectly justified, when we feel belittled, when we feel alone, or when evil has been done to us and we have little desire to return good in its place.

With hearts humbly knit together with unity and love, we can be a mighty force for good in our homes, in the Church, in our work, and in the world. When the tempests are nearly swamping our boat, our humbled hearts can find peace, comfort, and joy in being one with Christ and with our sisters in the gospel.

The Joseph City ward choir of my childhood sang it this way: "Perverse and foolish, oft I strayed, but yet in love He sought me, and on His shoulder gently laid and home rejoicing brought me. . . . I nothing lack [for] I am His, and He is mine forever."[5] I take comfort in God's promises to us, that his grace is sufficient, his burden is light, and he can give us rest.

NOTES

1. Armand L. Mauss, "Sociological Perspectives on the Mormon Subculture," *Annual Review of Sociology* 10 (1984): 437–60.

2. Ezra Taft Benson, "Beware of Pride," *Ensign,* May 1989, 4–7.

3. Lisa Flindt, untitled journal assignment from class, Brigham Young University, N442 Journal, Fall 1994; used with permission; slightly edited.

4. Dale LeBaron, ed., *All Are Alike unto God* (Salt Lake City: Bookcraft, 1990), 70–71.

5. Harry Rowe Shelley, "The King of Love My Shepherd Is," in *Sing unto God: Anthems and Sacred Choruses,* ed. and arr. by Ruth Heller (Minneapolis: Schmitt, Hall, & McCreary, 1952), 58–63; capitals at line breaks omitted.

TRACKING DOWN THE PRINCIPLES

MARY HALES

Trials are part of mortality. Some are no-fault trials, like no-fault insurance: through no fault of our own, we will suffer, things will go wrong. Our mortal bodies begin to break down from the day we are born, little by little, part by part. And the bodies of those we care about do, too. As quickly as we learn how to do one thing, conditions change. Our memory goes, our sight goes, our hearing goes. Once we are past seventy, we find our foyer visiting at church includes an organ recital: pancreas doesn't work, kidneys don't function, heart is clogged. That is just life.

How do we deal with what faces us? There is no way the Lord can give us enough laws to fit every possibility. The Israelites tried that. It doesn't work. Instead, he gives us principles, which he wants us to apply to our particular situation. That may take some figuring out because our problems and even our pleasures differ. Sometimes we struggle to see the principle and bog down in the details. For instance, at a recent women's conference, a speaker mentioned that she had taken a loaf of freshly baked bread to her new neighbor. She told how much good it did. A lot of people in that audience heard the word *bread* (I was one of them), and we said to ourselves,

---

Mary Hales, who received her bachelor's degree from Brigham Young University in home and family development, is a homemaker. She and her husband, Robert D. Hales, a member of the Quorum of the Twelve Apostles, are the parents of two children and the grandparents of eight. Mary teaches the Spiritual Living lessons in her ward Relief Society.

But I don't bake bread. The principle here, though, is not *take bread to your neighbor.* The principle is *show caring to your neighbor.*

When I lived in the East, I decided to make a Boston cream pie for a new neighbor. Boston cream pie is a misnomer; it's really a cake split into layers with pudding in between. To keep the top and bottom from slipping, you quickly insert toothpicks through the layers, slide the whole thing into the refrigerator, and hope it sets up straight. Once it's set, you frost it fast and hurry it back to the fridge before it starts to move. It's difficult to make, time consuming, and terribly messy. But it was a family favorite, and I thought, A new neighbor—I'll take her something special.

So I knocked on her door and said as I extended the Boston cream pie, "I'm your new neighbor. I brought you this to welcome you to our neighborhood." She looked at it and said, "Our family doesn't eat dessert." I said, "Oh." At home later, after I recovered from the shock of rejection, I said to myself, You know, she's right. I didn't think this out very well. What could I have taken this new neighbor I had never met? Not what does my family like, but what does she need? She needs my name and phone number so she can call and ask me when the trash is picked up or the name of a dentist for when her child wakes in the night with a toothache. There are things she needs that I could provide.

This same principle of caring by thinking of another's particular needs shows up in a ward. When did you last hear a baby cry in church? Probably last Sunday, because we expect babies and mothers to attend church. When a mother has small children, to survive she develops a tolerance for noise. She learns to distinguish the different cries of her child. Answering the cry that says *I'm tired,* she says, "Okay, I'll put you to bed"; to the cry that says *I'm hungry,* "Okay, I'll feed you"; to the *I'm just restless* cry, "I'll let you exercise your lungs a minute." When the child in sacrament meeting cries, he's probably tired.

The alarm in her head doesn't ring Emergency! Emergency! She registers, Ahh, it's a tolerable level, and goes about her business of listening to the speaker. The other members of the congregation, however, are alarmed. Those with hearing aids may be in pain.

How do we sort this out? First, a young mother deserves a gold star for even getting to church with a baby and diaper bag and everything else she needs. There has to be compromise on all sides. The mother has to listen with the ears of the congregation and say, "I know that I can tolerate a certain level of noise, but many in this congregation have forgotten or never experienced what it is like to have a child around. I have to consider their feelings." Others seated near her fussy baby have to say, "I will consider her needs. I will be supportive." Caring is the principle here; peace and quiet are secondary.

Our church is a lay church. That means we learn how to live the gospel by practicing it on each other. The choir learns to sing by singing. Will it be the best music you have ever heard? Probably not, but restrain yourself from screaming "Blend! Blend!" Choir volunteers come together to worship the Lord through music. It's not meant to be perfect music. When children give talks or offer fledgling testimonies, we rarely hear something we haven't heard before, but do we complain? Of course not. Bishops learn how to be bishops by practicing on us. Relief Society presidents learn how to be Relief Society presidents by practicing on us. We all take a turn. That's okay, because the Lord has told us to forgive and be patient with each other.

The world expects teachers to be specialists. The math teacher presumably knows far more than the vast majority of her students. The science teacher specializes in her course material. But in the Church, our fellow members teach classes. Fellow members give talks. Fellow members prepare to teach Gospel Doctrine or priesthood or Relief Society, often worrying themselves sick because they don't know any more than anyone else. In the Church, we are not specialists.

Where do we get the idea that other people are specialists? If we're assigned a topic, we do the best we can and try to teach with some enthusiasm so people will be interested and motivated. But that doesn't mean we've perfected the topic. We all feel depressed when we make comparisons. We all feel discouraged at times because we don't measure up to so-and-so. Everyone is struggling; everyone is learning.

If you don't think someone has trials, you just don't know the person well enough. The fact that some individuals can look on the bright side of life doesn't mean everything that happens to them is good or that they have life all figured out. They don't. No one does. The April 1995 *Harvard Mental Health Letter* reported some studies on perception, comparing optimists with pessimists. According to the study, optimists overestimate their own social skills and the amount of control they have over the outcome of events, but they accurately estimate other people. Pessimists' perceptions were reversed. They did not underestimate their own skills, as you might expect, but rather overestimated everyone else's. Both groups would benefit from the truth: the ability to see themselves and others accurately.[1] Our goal is to have realistic expectations.

Expect to have trials. The good news is you can cope with these trials with the help of the Lord and the help of your family and friends. But don't get the idea that tomorrow your trials will be gone. I once had the illusion that I would some day get my entire house cleaned. There would come a day when all at the same time, every room, every floor, every closet, every drawer would be clean all at once. But it's never going to happen, never, not in this world, not with me. If I get one thing in order or fixed, something else goes down. That's just how it is. But once I realized that and quit getting all upset about it, I learned to function. It's the same with life. I know the trials will come. Absolutely guaranteed, there will be trials.

16

So when they arise, I don't say, "Oh dear me, a trial!" I say, "Oh, another trial. Well, I coped with the last one. I'll cope with this one." That's how I go through life and keep my sanity.

Trials can be made worse if we burden ourselves with unrealistic expectations. For instance, when we think we didn't get anything out of a meeting, we need to reflect on why we go to church. The reality is we don't go to church to *get*. The Lord commanded us to go to sacrament meeting so that we could *give* our worship, *renew* our covenant to keep his commandments, and *support* and love each other. Every person who walks through that chapel door should feel the caring of other ward members. A sister can teach a lesson, and if we come up and talk to her afterward, she feels encouraged. I can sit in class and if I say, "How are you? How's it going? How is this problem, that problem?" she knows someone cares about her. We go to church to support each other, to show caring. If we have the realistic idea that we go to church to give and then we give, we will never be disappointed.

We need to carry that realism into our expectations of ourselves. There's a principle involved here, stated by King Benjamin in Mosiah 4:27: "See that all these things are done in wisdom and order." We are not required to run faster than we have strength. The quantity of good things we can do in a day is unlimited, but energy and resources are limited. A General Authority I know stayed with a family while on an out-of-town Church assignment. The family got up early to have family prayer together and scripture study before breakfast. That night he joined them as they studied scriptures and prayed together again before they went to bed. As their little boy rose from his knees to head off to bed, he blurted out, "Dad, what's going on?" Now that's life; that's the reality.

Because our time and energy are limited, we have to decide what is right for us and our family at a particular time of our life. We can look around and get ideas and suggestions about how others spend their time, but only we can decide what's right for us at this moment, and in what proportion. We need to commit ourselves—keep all the commandments—but allot our time according to our phase of life.

Not long ago I heard a woman speak in sacrament meeting about family history. It was a wonderful talk. She said, "I spend four hours a day on family history, and I love it." Is that wrong? Not for her. Her children are grown. She has the time. She loves it. It's doing good for other people. Are four hours right for everybody? For some, yes; for some, no. Who decides? You decide. If you go to a meeting and hear, "I spend four hours on family history," do you say, "Oh, woe is me. I'm depressed." No, you say, "I'm glad I heard that talk. She talked about what was really important in family history. I learned which things I need to throw in a drawer so that when I do have time, I won't have lost irreplaceable items. I'm glad I heard that talk. I'll let it help me, not depress me because I can't devote the hours to it this woman can." If someone makes the mistake of challenging you to work on family history four hours a day, just forgive that person. It's all right.

What if you want to try something new but have no way to fit it into your life? You say, "One more straw, and this camel is down." Don't keep piling on more and more responsibilities until you break. Instead consider, "What straw am I willing to remove for now so I can add this new straw?" or "What half of a straw here and another half straw there can I drop because I want to try this new straw for a while?" Exchange and keep exchanging as your life changes and as you change. Keep adjusting your time and commitments to fit your personal needs.

In all this juggling and adjusting of expectations, in accepting our own and others' limitations, things happen to us that are positively unfair as well as painful. Some people say, "Well, what principles will work here? Prayer! I'll pray it away. I'll fast and I'll pray and I know the Lord will take this away." But that's not a true principle. Look at the example of the Savior when he went to Gethsemane. What was fair about his atonement? He understood what atonement was, how painful it would be. He even asked his Father in Heaven, "Can this cup pass from me?" In other words, can this trial be removed? But he added, "Thy will, Lord, not mine." Did the Lord remove the trial? No, he did not. What did he do? He strengthened his Son.

Some of us will have trials that will be more than we feel we can bear. We'll say, "I want it removed. It's too much." The Lord will respond, "I'll strengthen you."

My husband and I are good friends with an energetic, bright, enthusiastic young couple who have three young children. Their future was full of promise. Then the husband began to notice a strange numbness in his hand. He consulted a doctor, who conducted some tests, did some surgery, and then some more tests. Soon afterward the doctor told them the tests indicated Lou Gehrig's disease. This is a very young family; Lou Gehrig's disease doesn't usually hit someone so young. Now this man can no longer walk or talk. Only his wife can understand him, and sometimes even she can't. The children climb up on his lap to hug him. I look at this young family and wonder how they can stand what's happening to them.

The illness isn't something that runs its course quickly; it takes several years. The ward has been very helpful. They built a ramp to his home so that he can come out in his wheelchair. His extended family members help and support him in every way possible. But it's extremely painful to watch. I asked the young mother one day how she was coping because I couldn't imagine how she could. She said, "Well, the day before we returned to the doctor we went to the temple to prepare ourselves for the diagnosis, which we suspected was going to be very serious. There in the temple, a peace and a strengthening came over us, and it has stayed with us ever since." She added, "That doesn't mean we don't get bone tired and we don't cry from the sorrow of what's happening, but we are strengthened

19

and that has stayed with us since we found out what was wrong." Pain in this life is not a sign that the Lord is angry or that we have done wrong. It's just mortality.

The gospel teaches principles based on eternal truths. As we identify the principle involved in our choices, we develop the ability to cope successfully with the trials of mortality. Gospel principles teach us to value caring about others over personal irritation as we weed out unrealistic expectations of ourselves and others. We need to develop realistic expectations softened with compassion. If we learn to yield our will to the Father's and pray the way the Savior showed us—"Thy will be done"—then he will bless us with the understanding that even those trying to do right will experience trials. We will know the Lord loves us and allow him to strengthen us as we strengthen and care for each other.

NOTE

1. Lauren B. Alloy, "Depressive Realism: Sadder but Wiser?" *Harvard Mental Health Letter,* Apr. 1995, 4–5.

WHY I LOVE THE BRETHREN

ALICE A. WARNER

Like you, I have had occasion to think about the way Christ governs his Church and the Saints who belong to it. I am not in a position to correct or to preach. I intend simply to offer my testimony, to tell you why I love the Brethren as I do.

THE LORD'S ORDER

History proves over and over the dangers of succumbing to those who desire power over others. The quest for control has brought about the world's greatest evils in nations, in schools, in homes. These devastating evils have given rise to many prevailing social ideas such as these: Life is what you make it, so take control of your life; you're in charge. To be happy, be yourself. Honor your own feelings, whatever they may be. You will lose your identity, your true self, if you defer to the authority or direction of others. So assert yourself, defend yourself, stand for yourself.

This is not a new philosophy. Korihor, the great anti-Christ of the Book of Mormon, advocated this position very convincingly (Alma 30:12–28). He warned believers not "*to bind themselves down under the foolish ordinances*" (v. 23). He said the priests would try to "*usurp power and authority over them, to keep them in ignorance*" (v. 23). So, he admonished, don't be

Alice A. Warner graduated from Brigham Young University and is president and CEO of an international management consulting firm. Alice served a mission in Taiwan and enjoys her calling as choir director.

taken in by the idea of an atonement—a grand design in which we prosper through obedience, humility, and submission. Instead, Korihor taught, everyone will fare in this life according to his or her own genius and strength; in effect, assert yourself, defend yourself, stand for yourself.

Korihor's doctrine makes perfect sense in a world without a loving Heavenly Father, a redeeming Savior, or a divine order ordained and authorized by them for the purpose of saving us. But in a world with a Father, a Savior, and their holy Church, bending our will to a higher order will indeed save us, not endanger us.

The Lord's order is different in nature from any earthly system of governance or authority. This order is reflected in Christ's relationship to his Father. "For I came down from heaven," he said, "not to do mine own will, but the will of him that sent me" (John 6:38). In this and other scriptures like it, Christ made clear that he has a will of his own, but his choice—for him a life choice—was to turn his will over to the Father. In other words, then and now his position of authority derives not from the pursuit of power but from the spirit of submissiveness.

This divine order extends to special witnesses, revelators, and seers. Like the Savior's position with the Father, their position is one of submission and discipleship. They, too, are called upon to say, "Not as I will, but as thou wilt" (Matthew 26:39). They have no authority or power independent of their personal willingness to submit, heart and soul, to those who direct and guide *them*. For this reason, their authority differs fundamentally from all other forms of authority in any institution or society on earth of which I know. Their authority is not born of a quest to dominate; it is a by-product of their quest to obey.

PERFECTION IS NOT A PREREQUISITE

It is easy to minimize the connection between submitting ourselves to Christ and obeying the Brethren. "Christ," we may say, "was perfect, but the Brethren are just human."

22

Many of us are now parents or someday will be. This is a very serious responsibility. The physical and spiritual lives of pure little children are or will be entrusted to us as parents. Perhaps perfection should be a prerequisite for such a lofty undertaking. Suppose that is what our children expected of us. The moment they believed we had made a mistake, they would feel no obligation to honor or sustain us anymore. Furthermore, they would feel compelled to advertise our shortcomings, convincing the other children that they need not obey either. It would be impossible to have a family under such circumstances.[1]

I was fifteen when I discovered my mother was not perfect. (I gave my dad a slightly longer grace period.) As I get older, I see more clearly their weaknesses and their defects—in part because I share so many of them. Did their humanness make them unworthy parents? Of course not. In fact, that they did what they did for me, *in* all of their humanness, affirms in my mind that Heavenly Father called them to oversee my upbringing. He upheld them, he taught them, and he compensated for their frailties. Perfection is not a prerequisite to parenthood.

We may feel inclined to make the Brethren's perfection a condition of our loyalty, to lay hold upon perceived shortcomings as an excuse for disobedience. On occasion, we may even be tempted to share a morsel of gossip or levy a criticism or spread a rumor that would diminish one of them. Whether the tidbit is true or not (and how would we know anyway?) is irrelevant. For if our hearts are right, we may discover that we are trying to justify our own sins. It's as though casting doubt on *their* worthiness relieves us of *our* obligation to obey. But it doesn't. Their defects, real or perceived, do not weaken the covenants we have made to follow them.

The Savior himself instituted the plan that authorizes certain human beings to represent him. He who is perfect must have noticed that *they* aren't. And still he called them. Far from making the Lord's plan questionable, this fact—that he anoints

23

human beings to lead us—is a testament of his power to sanctify and to enlarge. That the Brethren do what they do for us, *in* their humanness, affirms in my mind that the Lord stands by them. He upholds them, he teaches them, and he compensates for their frailties. Perfection is not a prerequisite to ordination.

THE BURDEN OF LEADERSHIP

I have managed a consulting company for the past several years. Recently, in a reflective moment, I was struck by the virtue and nobility of my extraordinary colleagues. How absurd that I was trying to lead them! Overwhelmed with feelings of inadequacy, I considered resigning. Only two days later, I happened upon the following: "We who have been called to lead the church are ordinary men and women with ordinary capacities. . . . Some are disposed to find fault with us; surely that is easy for them to do. But they do not examine us more searchingly than we examine ourselves. . . . We are sorry for our inadequacies, sorry we are not better than we are."[2] I don't want to trivialize the holy position of the Brethren by comparing it with my own, but it is the closest I can come to identifying, even in a small way, with what they must feel.

How would I feel if the next time I accepted a call, my bishop said, "Now, there are nine million good-hearted people depending upon you, Alice. Your every word and action will be thoroughly scrutinized. They will look to you for guidance about the conduct of their lives. If you make a mistake, it may adversely affect their devotion and faith. And, by the way, I hope you haven't made any mistakes up to this point in your life—no gold-digging, no careless word, no giving of the slightest offense—or you may be roundly criticized. Your effectiveness in this role will depend upon your humble receptivity to inspiration and revelation. Thus, every choice you make must enhance your worthiness in every way. You will spend the rest of your life working full time under this burden, going where you are asked, when you are asked, doing exactly what you are asked." What kind of person would the Lord entrust with such a challenge? What kind of person could meet it?

AND NO MAN TAKETH THIS HONOUR . . .

In answer, I would like to share a few stories about the lives of the Brethren. These are sacred stories, and I tell them with reverence.

A few years ago, I worked in a large, high-profile, international company on the East Coast. My boss, the founder and CEO of the company, was brilliant, eccentric, argumentative—and typically impervious to what is spiritually discerned. Twice he had occasion to meet with Elder Henry B. Eyring. After the first meeting, he reported that he had never met such a humble person and that he felt honored to be in Elder Eyring's presence. He said, "It never occurred to me, Alice, that humility could be impressive." After the second meeting, he told me in a quiet moment that Henry Eyring's goodness made him want to be good. Yet, despite a long track record of affecting people in this way, when Elder Eyring was called to the apostleship, he seemed taken by surprise. He told us in his conference address, weeping, that during the hours between his private call and his public sustaining, he had "learned some things about [humility]."[3] *"And no man taketh this honour unto himself, but he that is called of God"* (Hebrews 5:4). *"And before honour is humility"* (Proverbs 15:33).

Elder Neal A. Maxwell performed the marriage of my brother and his wife. He knows neither of them well, yet when he heard years later about their struggle with infertility, he offered to travel to their home to give a priesthood blessing. When asked how he could find time in his heavy schedule to visit distant acquaintances in need, he explained that he was called to minister and was merely fulfilling that call. *"Whosoever will be chief among you, let him be your servant"* (Matthew 20:27).

Elder Marcus Helvécio Martins, the Church's first black

General Authority, was living with his wife in Brazil when plans for the São Paulo temple were announced. Because of his lineage, Elder Martins was not permitted to hold the priesthood at that time. His devoted service to the Church during those years is miraculous to me. But there is more. He and his wife sold their jewelry to contribute to the building of a temple they could not enter. *"And thus they have been called to this holy calling on account of their faith"* (Alma 13:4).

Not many years ago, President Howard W. Hunter lost the use of his legs. The loss, he was told, was permanent. But he felt he could not carry on effectively if he couldn't walk. So, against advice, he began an intensive rehabilitation program that a family member described to me as physically excruciating. This he did so that he could serve us better and longer. This he did in behalf of our salvation. *"Obey them that have the rule over you, and submit yourselves: for they watch for your souls"* (Hebrews 13:17).

Can I resist such love for me? Can I criticize such devotion? Must I worry about defending myself in the face of such goodness?

OBEDIENCE IS NEVER BLIND

I have noticed that despite clear scriptural warnings about its consequences, Korihor's beguiling doctrine has a way of sneaking up on us. We get nervous about being in charge of our lives. We worry that followership will strip us of our identity, that submission may rob us of our intellect. Such self-concern draws us away from the warmth of the Lord's light.

About four months before the end of my mission in Taiwan, I was working in an area where we had many baptisms, many who had committed to baptism, and a promising pool of investigators. I expected to finish my mission in this spot. We had planned a wonderful Christmas Nativity program with the ward members and our many investigators, complete with costumes and readings and music. On the afternoon of

December 24, my mission president called. An elder who had developed feelings for a sister missionary had requested a transfer. But, my president explained, Elder William R. Bradford, our area president in Hong Kong, felt that the elder should not leave his important leadership position. So, rather than transfer the elder, he requested that I and another sister switch places. I was to board a train that very evening, unaccompanied, to the most unproductive part of the mission, where I would finish out my service. I was shocked and discouraged. My roommates and companion were downright angry. Our mission president was provincial, they said. And what about Elder Bradford—what was he doing interfering like that? These men marginalize women! Just because we don't have priesthood callings—does that make us completely interchangeable? What about the ward Christmas program? I was responsible for the music and piano accompaniment. What about my investigators? I couldn't say good-bye or explain. I would just disappear, and some other sister would step in—as if no one would notice or care! With a heavy and confused heart, I packed my clothes, books, and a copy of our little Nativity script and boarded the train. I didn't want to feel bitter, but this turn of events was just too much to swallow with a smile on my face.

My new companion and two elders greeted me at the station when I arrived that evening. The first thing they asked was if I knew anything about music. The next day was Christmas, and the branch members wanted to stage a Christmas program like ones they had heard of in the established city wards. But neither they nor the other missionaries had any idea how to do it.

We went immediately to the small branch meeting rooms. All twenty branch members and some investigators were gathered, looking in library books to see what people in Israel wear. But discouragement was setting in, for the Israeli attire didn't resemble anything they might pick up at the local

Chinese clothing market! Drawing on my years as the orchestrator of the Warner family Christmas pageant, I helped the members and investigators round up robes and towels, shepherd canes, and cardboard crowns. Copying the little script I had tucked in my suitcase didn't take long. We practiced our songs—even learned parts—and on Christmas shared the most worshipful evening of praise and remembrance I have ever experienced. Thus began the best months of my mission and some of the happiest of my life.

It doesn't always turn out this way; I don't always so readily see purpose in what I am asked to do. In fact, I have received—and followed—instructions about my life from Church leaders that still don't make perfect sense to me. But even when I don't fully understand why the instruction has come or what its consequences might be, I believe that humble obedience is still the right course.

I've heard people say, "Well, that's just blind obedience." *Blind obedience.* Those words imply following with no thought, no consideration, no inspiration, no insight. For me, to dismiss obedience as blind is to misunderstand what obedience is. Every moment a choice is presented to us: "How will I use my agency in this moment?" When I choose to obey or to submit, I have not blindly abdicated my freedom to choose. Rather, I have used it to choose the Lord.

In my experience, obedience to Church leaders requires more insight, wisdom, and thought than resistance. I obey because I see that there is a Christ who lived to redeem me. I obey because I see that my redemption, from moment to moment, depends upon giving myself to him and to his servants. I obey because I see that there is an atonement and that I stand in need of its purifying power. I obey because I see that this purifying power flows through his divine priesthood order, of which obedience makes me a part. I obey because of what I see, not because of what I am blind to.

TO WALK IN HIS LIGHT

It is easy to confuse worldly rhetoric with eternal truths. We may fear that if we obey in meekness and humility, our heads will be kept down, as Korihor said, and the flame of our identity will be snuffed out (see Alma 30:23). So we go about trying to create our own light—in the name of individual rights, or intellectualism, or self-assertiveness, or some other cause independent of the great cause of Christ. But the very act of trying to kindle our own light separates us from the Lord's, convincing us further that there is not enough for us in his divine order.

Here's how Isaiah said it: "Behold, all ye that kindle a fire, that compass yourselves about with sparks: walk in the light of your fire, and in the sparks that ye have kindled. This shall ye have of mine hand; ye shall lie down in sorrow" (Isaiah 50:11).

Walking in the light of the Lord's divine order requires that we abandon the security of our own meager flame. President Harold B. Lee taught that to find the Lord's light, we must walk to the edge of ours and even a few steps into the darkness. We cannot at the same time stand in the flicker of our own willful sparks and bask in the warmth of his magnificent light.

The times in my life when I feel most whole, most liberated, most free, most *me,* are the times when my whole being is filled with the desire to stand not for myself but for and with the Brethren. I give up only my self-concern, my resistance, and my pride—and they aren't me. Gentleness, peace, and a willing heart take their place.

When I stand squarely in the light of the Lord's direction, it's as though all of my faculties, enhanced by the Spirit, come alive with insight and vision and clarity. There is no longer a distinction between the intellectual and the spiritual. That is the closest I have come to experiencing what Paul calls having "the mind of Christ" (1 Corinthians 2:16). That is the closest I have come to feeling my body full of the light, pure and penetrating, that comes when my eye is single to him (see Matthew 6:22).

As Mordecai explained to Esther when what she was asked to do seemed too difficult for her, if we refuse to obey, the Lord will find other ways of carrying out his purpose. Our soul, not his work, will suffer. Who knows but what we were come "for such a time as this" (Esther 4:14)—a time of great divisiveness and very tempting ideas, a time when obedience and submissiveness are derided as weak and unthinking, and a time when our salvation will depend upon our willingness to follow anyway. May we not be deceived. May we see and think as clearly as Christ when he yielded his will to *his* leader. May bending our will to our leaders, those chosen of the Lord and upheld by him, be our quest, and may our hearts be drawn out to them in submission, loyalty, and love.

NOTES

1. I am indebted to my friend and colleague Duane Boyce for suggesting this analogy in his article "The Brethren and the Lord: A Letter to My Children," *This People,* Fall 1995, 34–46. Both his article and his friendship significantly influenced this essay.

2. Boyd K. Packer, "Revelation in a Changing World," *Ensign,* Nov. 1989, 16.

3. Henry B. Eyring, "Always Remember Him," *Ensign,* May 1995, 25.

THE ART OF COMPASSION, THE COMPASSION OF ART

ELIZABETH HANSEN

The more I learn about compassion, the more I am inclined to believe that it is an art, something to be experienced, examined, and yearned for. But what is compassion exactly? How does it differ from sympathy, concern, or pity? Compassion is a deep awareness of the suffering of another *coupled with the wish to relieve that suffering.* Compassion must be more active than mere sympathy. But how do we come to that deeper awareness? I believe that empathy leads the heart toward compassion.

Empathy is the capacity to experience, as your own, the feelings of another. But how can we as humans, with our temporal limitations, climb into another's soul to feel that person's life firsthand? Can we become Jews in a concentration camp? Can we become an AIDS victim and realize the terror of facing death? Can we rejoice at the finding of true love, only then to lose it? I believe we can. We can transcend our own realm into another's and fly alongside their soul through art. We can be a name on *Schindler's List,* can visit *Philadelphia,* or stand in the *Shadowlands.* Perhaps the flight is short, perhaps it will

Elizabeth Hansen teaches play writing and screenwriting at BYU. She received her master of fine arts degree in screenwriting from the American Film Institute and has won a Writers Guild of America Award and an Emmy nomination for her television writing. Also a performer, she has been seen on Broadway, toured nationally, and appeared with such performers as Carol Channing, Milton Berle, James Mason, and Rudolf Nureyev.

provide only a momentary glance, but without that glance, we may miss the opportunity to taste the abundance of compassion.

Christ admonished us, "Love your enemies, do good to them which hate you, bless them that curse you, and pray for them which despitefully use you" (Luke 6:27–28). Could he have asked this of us if he had not tasted mortality?

How easy it is to condemn and judge when one is without the experience of living. "There is nothing heavier than compassion. Not even one's own pain weighs so heavy as the pain one feels *with* someone, *for* someone, a pain intensified by the imagination and prolonged by a hundred echoes," says Czech writer Milan Kundera in *The Unbearable Lightness of Being*.[1] God knew and understood that truth firsthand, and he sent his Son to experience it for himself. Christ in the garden took upon himself the full weight of human misery and error in the ultimate act of compassion. But unlike Christ, our experience as humans is limited to our own time and space. How do we push the boundaries of what we know? How do we learn compassion?

I recently came across the diary entry of a fourteen-year-old girl:

"April 12, 1969

"Today, I went to see *Ben Hur*. Well, that was the best show that I have ever seen. It was very gory, and yet it was so beautiful. It taught you to be thankful that you live in this time and place.

"It was about Judah Ben Hur (Charleton Heston) and how he was taken to the galleys and his mother and sister were imprisoned. On his way to the galleys he met Jesus. Jesus gave him water when he was not to have any. Ben Hur never forgot him or his face. When Ben Hur got back to Judea, Esther told him that his mother and sister were dead, but they weren't. They were leopards [sic]. They had gone to the valley of the leopards.

"So he went there and found Esther bringing some food to his mother and sister. After that Esther went to the sermon on the mount and saw Jesus. She told Ben Hur and they both went to the valley of the leopards to get his mother and sister to take them to see Jesus, but Jesus was going to be crucified. And when Jesus died the place went dark and it rained hard and Esther went and had to take Miriam and his sister into a cave for protection and they got well.

"They were so happy, it was sad. He told Esther about when Jesus had said, 'Father forgive them for they know not what they do.' And said that Christ's words had pulled the sword out of his hand. When you saw all of Jesus' blood in the rain and in the stream it was so sad, everybody was just crying their eyes out. It was such a good movie. I felt so good inside to know that Jesus died so that we might live.

"I make a vow. That I will try to keep. I will never make fun of my religion again. Or about Jews. Bye."

I'm afraid that I haven't always kept that vow. But I remember writing those words. I remember where I was, and how I felt. I was only fourteen. I didn't know a leper from a leopard. But that movie had a powerful effect on my heart and mind, which is still readily available. How can we instill compassion into another's heart? By first finding our own. And the arts can help.

As I teach students in my screenwriting and playwrighting classes, I explain that a story is an account or a recital of an event or series of events, incidents, or experiences, either true or fictitious, intended to interest or amuse the hearer or reader. More succinctly, a story is a series of events in which one person acts upon someone else *and we find out why*. That's the important part, the part that hooks us in. It is the story, then, that engages us, interests us, involves us—just as it is the plight of an individual or group that moves us to compassion.

Story may, then, be the gateway to compassion. Because when we become swept up in a story, we care if E.T. phones home, or if Dorothy gets back to Kansas, or if the Phantom of the Opera finds his soul amid his own emotional desolation and releases the virtuous Christine from his maniacal grasp. If in theater, film, poetry, or literature, story is indeed the gateway to compassion, then what happens when we venture outside the fictitious into the real world? Perhaps through considering fictitious circumstances, we can better understand those real stories and relationships of people we know, so that we care that our best friend has lost a homosexual brother, or we feel for a loved one who is an alcoholic, or we even recognize that we can be kinder to ourselves when we are not as good a parent as we wish we were. Through the channel of storytelling, we can learn to exercise compassion.

In the film *It's a Wonderful Life,* we care that a man, pushed to the limit, with nowhere to turn, looks to suicide to solve his problems. We care what happens to him, and because we do, we have compassion for him. In the final scenes of the movie *Schindler's List,* Oscar Schindler has saved more than fifteen hundred Jews from the gas chambers. Yet ridden with guilt and remorse, Schindler agonizes that he didn't save more people. He wasted so much money. If he had only sold his Nazi pin, he could have saved one more. If he had sold his car, he could have saved maybe two. In anguish, Schindler collapses into the arms of a Jewish friend and weeps. We can feel Oscar Schindler's deep, inconsolable grief at not having saved more people. We can empathize with his circumstances, even though we have not actually experienced them ourselves: his anguish reaches our own feelings of sorrow, and we care deeply about him. Having exercised these feelings of compassion and caring through film and theater, we will be more likely to experience those emotions when someone around us is hurting or in despair.

To show compassion you do not have to—indeed, you cannot—experience every situation firsthand. You don't have to have been in a concentration camp or near suicide; you don't have to be a direct participant in your neighbor's grief to feel compassion. You just have to be willing to see the suffering, empathize with it, and want to do something about it.

Reflect on Christ in the garden, taking upon himself the sins of the world. Perhaps afterward he understood as never before our unique plight as humans. Empathy is essential for compassion, because it leads us not only to pity but to *understand* why people are as they are. And, in the words of Alexander Chase, "To understand is to forgive, even oneself."[2]

In my life, art and compassion are intertwined. Art, in all its forms, is the only temporal element that can lift me from the drudgery of mortal existence to catch a glimpse of God. "I can't tell you what art does and how it does it," says John Berger, British author and critic, "but I know that often art has judged the judges, pleaded revenge to the innocent, and shown to the future what the past suffered, so that it has never been forgotten."[3]

On the other hand, just as film has the power to teach tolerance and compassion, so can it also teach hatred and cruelty. The Nazis understood well the power of the media during World War II and used it to influence and poison the minds of German citizens against Jews, Poles, Czechs, Gypsies, homosexuals, the mentally disabled, and any person, religion, ethic, or ideal that those in power found contrary to Nazi doctrine. The Nazis came to believe their own propaganda and in so doing slaughtered innocent millions, both temporally and spiritually. Art gone awry can be deadly in more than just the literal sense. It can deaden our senses and our souls to human suffering. It can persuade and influence us to accept and even delight in that cruelty.

Unfortunately, much contemporary art reflects the worst of modern society. What I see is a group of artists out of touch with human virtues trying to justify their self-indulgences. Too much of art has become, in the words of cartoonist Al Capp, "a product of the untalented sold by the unprincipled to the utterly bewildered."[4]

How and why does an artist choose to persuade hearts toward compassion rather than toward immorality, hatred, or self-indulgence? I'm not sure I can answer that question, but I do know that if we want to live in a more gentle, compassionate world, our goal should not be to eliminate art but to retrench it, to support it in its most compassionate and purest form. Truthful art has the power to bless us, inspire us, and impel us to do good works. Says Austrian poet and critic Ernst Fischer, "In a decaying society, art, if it is truthful, must also reflect decay. And unless it wants to break faith with its social function, art must show the world as changeable. And help to change it."[5]

That is what art must do—not simply reflect a "decaying society" but help change society. Art must help move people to compassion, tolerance, and love, not to intolerance and hate. It must foster goodwill, not ungodliness. Art—theater, film, music, painting, poetry—can and should impel us towards hope and school us in compassion.

NOTES

1. Milan Kundera, *The Unbearable Lightness of Being* (New York: Harper & Row, 1984), quoted in *The Columbia Dictionary of Quotations,* as found on Bookshelf '94 (Microsoft Home, Columbia University Press, 1993).

2. Alexander Chase, in *The International Thesaurus of Quotations,* s.v. "Understanding Others."

3. John Berger, *Keeping a Rendezvous* (1992), quoted in *Columbia Dictionary of Quotations.*

4. Al Capp, *National Observer* (Silver Spring, Md., 1 July 1963), quoted in *Columbia Dictionary of Quotations.*

5. Ernst Fischer, "The Necessity of Art" (1959; trans. 1963), quoted in *Columbia Dictionary of Quotations.*

WHY I BELIEVE

BONNIE D. PARKIN

The month of March was crazy. I was still getting over the shock of my new calling and stressing over my talk for the General Young Women meeting when, a week before the broadcast, I walked into my office and found a letter from the First Presidency. Could it be a pink slip?

I ripped open the envelope to discover my worst nightmare realized: I was to speak in the closing session of general conference in three weeks. I wept, phoned my husband, and was sure I'd have diarrhea for the rest of the month!

During an early morning walk, I discussed with some close friends the daunting subject of why we believe. Their responses were like mine: It's too scary not to! After all, facing life with its paradoxes, complexities, and unanswerable questions is difficult enough *with* God in the equation. None of us could, or was willing to, imagine living without God and, by extension, his church.

I think about my father's mother, Agnes Ruth Kunz Dansie, who had an incredibly hard life. The oldest of six children, she was nine years old when, as her mother was giving birth to a seventh child, both mother and child died. Agnes had to quit school, care for her younger brothers and sisters, and help run

Bonnie Dansie Parkin serves as second counselor in the Young Women General Presidency. She and her husband, James L. Parkin, are the parents of four strapping sons and four terrific daughters-in-law and the grandparents of four grandchildren.

the family dairy. It's a common story, familiar from the past of many of us.

When Agnes was eighteen, she married a man fourteen years her senior in an arranged marriage and moved to a small Utah town. Life was not easy. She raised children while she raised chickens. She ran her own dairy and supplemented that meager income by writing articles for the local *Midvale Sentinel*. She served as a Relief Society president, sent a son on a mission in Depression years, and, while he was gone, had another baby.

I remember her standing with me at a mirror helping me practice my Primary talks, gently correcting my mistakes and calming my anxious nerves. (I had stage fright even then.) I remember the way people spoke about her with admiration and love. Of course she wasn't perfect, but she gave her all to whatever she did; she brought a measure of culture, generosity, and love to a little town called Herriman.

Why would she *do* such things?

I never asked her. I do know, though, that she was a living example of belief; example initiates belief.

One morning my mother, at age eleven, sat talking to her mother as she brushed her hair. Suddenly her mother slumped to the floor. Soon afterward she died of a brain aneurism, leaving behind nine children. Devastated, my mother had plenty of excuses not to believe: What kind of God would take a young child's mother? But she pushed onward, living by her motto: "Do what is right; let the consequence follow."[1] I was born of goodly parents. I had ties to the Church; I was brought up with the gospel.

Women in our little town of Herriman gave a lot to make Primary meaningful. Back then, Primary was held in the middle of the week, and getting together was something I looked forward to. I remember we gave pennies to Primary Children's Hospital, had parades around the church parking lot, and sang songs. There in the old Herriman Ward, paintings of the prophets surrounded us, looking down on us, smiling, approving, reminding. There in that brick building, even at a very young age, I sang the words to Primary songs and felt a profound tenderness. It was as though I knew the Church was true.

Many times during my childhood, my mother was near death. Once she was hospitalized with heart disease for three months, and we were unable to go inside to visit her. We would go to the hospital and position ourselves on the lawn outside her window. Three months is a long time without a mother.

My mother and I received our patriarchal blessings together. We drove miles to another town to the home of an elderly patriarch who did not know either one of us. I was twenty-one, ready to graduate from college. Mother was forty-nine, but that wasn't too old to receive such a gift. Going for these blessings was one of the most powerful experiences of my life. I will never forget that day—how the patriarch placed his hands on Mother's head and told her how often her life had been spared—the rheumatic fever, the heart disease, the many illnesses. He recounted her life, enumerating the times she had blessed others' lives. He told her of other things the Lord had in store for her and told her of things she needed to do. It was as though we weren't sitting on chairs—we were raised up, lifted up, together. I knew her life, and this patriarch who didn't know her described her life.

This blessing was a witness to me that God lived, that he knew us individually, that he was there for us. It was a witness to me that the Church is true. I felt the existence of God and the power of the priesthood.

Why did my mother go to receive a patriarchal blessing so late in her life? Why did she spend so much of her life doing good, but not easy, things?

I'm only beginning to understand.

At my age, I realize that faith is a process, not an event. It's a warm sweater we're constantly growing into. Somehow I know that. While I am often impatient for my growth, I watch my tulips, planted in the fall, push their heads through thawing soil, and I know I too will continue to grow and bloom.

I think of John Thelwall, the nineteenth-century English radical, who thought it "unfair to influence a child's mind by inculcating any opinions before it should have come to years of discretion, and be able to choose for itself." There is an enlightening anecdote in Samuel Taylor Coleridge's *Table Talk:* "I showed [John Thelwall] my garden, and told him it was my botanical garden. 'How so?' said he, 'it is covered with weeds.'—'Oh,' I replied, '*that* is only because it has not yet come to its age of discretion and choice. The weeds, you see, have taken the liberty to grow, and I thought it unfair in me to prejudice the soil towards roses and strawberries.'"[2] My parents helped me pull the weeds so that somewhere I might have roses and strawberries and tulips.

I have friends who find believing difficult. It does not seem part of their nature. I am lucky. I was born with a believing heart. To say I haven't questioned would be untrue, but to be born with a believing heart is a blessing. And a part of that comes from my ancestry, members or not.

A convert friend of mine said to me: "You lifelong members were born with the gospel tree in your backyard. You enjoyed the shade of the tree, but some time or another, you have to know for yourself—like all converts. You have to climb that tree and experiment upon the word." To those who struggle to have a believing heart, remember Alma 32. You can experiment upon the word, you can feel it grow within you, you can taste its fruit and know that it is good, for "the fruit of the Spirit is love, joy, peace, longsuffering, gentleness, goodness, faith, meekness, temperance . . . " (Galatians 5:22–23).

I also believe because of you. Paul yearned for a time to join the Christian believers in Rome: "I long to see you . . . that I may be comforted together with you by the mutual faith both of you and me" (Romans 1:11–12). As I travel throughout the Church in my calling, I can scarcely contain my awe at your dedication, your struggles, your faith and charity, your testimonies.

Finally, there are moments when I don't have to ask myself why I believe. Spiritual whisperings come quietly, sometimes with years between them. But I remember those moments, like patriarchal blessings and Primary songs.

When I had to stand in the Tabernacle and give that general conference talk, I was very, very frightened. The Saturday night before I was to speak, my husband and sons gave me a blessing. It was comforting and assuring, but I did not sleep well. During the morning session of conference, my heart began its slow crescendo to my ascent of those steep stairs. I did not know how I would do it. Sister Pinegar said, "I looked at your husband on the front row, and he looked more nervous than you." I'm not sure that was possible.

Then just before my address, while Elder L. Tom Perry was speaking, I had a witness that I *could* give my talk—the Spirit enfolded my entire body like a celestial sweater. I thought of my grandmother standing with me beside a mirror, practicing a talk to make it perfect. And then I knew I could speak with the Spirit, and things would be okay—no matter how my husband looked. A peace fell over me; that stairway was shortened, and my troubled heart was calmed.

Why do I believe? I believe because of spiritual whisperings, because of a believing heart, because of you, because of goodly parents and grandparents. Because words cannot capture the soarings of my spirit.

I believe because amidst all these good and powerful things, I know that "eye hath not seen, nor ear heard, neither have entered into the heart of man, the things which God hath prepared for them that love him. But God hath revealed them unto us by his Spirit" (1 Corinthians 2:9–10).

NOTES

1. *Hymns of The Church of Jesus Christ of Latter-day Saints* (Salt Lake City: The Church of Jesus Christ of Latter-day Saints, 1985), no. 237.

2. William J. Bennett, *Book of Virtues* (New York: Simon & Schuster, 1993), 742.

THE INNER LIFE

JOANN SHIELDS

From the moment of quickening, you have had an inner life. Although your soul is complex and mysterious, the concept of the inner life is not. It's simply what goes on inside rather than outside your body. It's thoughts and feelings, the motives and emotions that govern action. The quality of inner life varies from person to person in much the same way the outer life does, except the two can be opposites. You can have an empty outer life and a full inner life, or vice versa. Corrie ten Boom defined the inner life as the life "we live . . . with God."[1] By praying and reading her smuggled hand-sized Bible, Corrie sustained a magnificent inner life with God even though her outer life in World War II death camps was hideous beyond imagining.

On this earth, most of us will never see the Lord with our outer eyes. In Doctrine and Covenants 38:7, he said his eyes are on us and he is among us but we cannot see him. We may all, however, see him with our *inner* eyes—which sight is just as real and just as soul changing. The inner life we live with God is filled with powerful thoughts and feelings he communicates to us through the Holy Ghost.

Let me explain what I mean by power in the inner life. *Power* means different things to different people. For some it means money: If I have enough money, I can do what I want

---

Joann Shields is a Salt Lake City attorney specializing in business litigation. She served a mission in Quebec, Canada, and is a member of the Young Women General Board.

when I want to. For others, it means fame: Everyone knows my name and loves my face. For far too many, it means control: I have power over others. I can boss people around and manipulate their choices and perceptions.

These definitions of power are made up by people who don't have any. They lack the only true power: godliness, or goodness. In Matthew 28:18 we read that all power in the heaven and earth is given to the Lord Jesus Christ, so we must look to him for the true source and definition of power.

God's power has nothing to do with money, fame, or control. In fact, Jesus repeatedly warned pleasers of men that they would never find him, his kingdom, or his power. To the moneymongers, Jesus said, "He that hath eternal life is rich" (D&C 6:7). To the fame seekers: "All honor comes from God. Before honor comes humility" (see John 5:44; Proverbs 15:33). To the control brokers: "Share power or lose it" (see D&C 121:37).

God's power in the inner life can be illustrated by a simple law of physics. Two soda pop cans, an empty one and an unopened full one, look exactly alike on the outside. But no matter how hard I try, I can't dent the full can, whereas with one squeeze I can crumple the empty can. The reason I can't dent the full can is that it has as much pressure inside as outside. The empty can has no internal pressure, so the external pressure crushes it. Although mortal beings cannot really be compared to pop cans, the analogy holds. We will collapse under relentless life stresses unless we have more power coming from within than pressure bearing down on us from without. We may, in fact, thrive under the constant pressures we all face, but we cannot do it alone. We were never meant to. Our burdens may become light, because Christ will carry them. He will give us the power—that is, the thoughts and feelings—to do everything we can, and then he will use his power to do everything we cannot. That's grace. God's power heals and nourishes the soul. It sustains the inner life. It gives humans the will to repent and overcome their natural, fallen state.

Last January I traveled to California with one of my friends, a savvy, brilliant, thirty-year-old lawyer who had been away from the Church several years. For nearly the entire trip, she vented examples of the soul-searing reason she left: spiritual aloneness. She was the only member in her family and never felt accepted in the Church family. Outside the Church she had found community and communion—some of it beyond the mark. My friend said she would never, never come back to the Church and subject herself again to such loneliness and non-stop rejection. I understood but after several painful hours couldn't sustain the grace to respond to her cry for compassion and connection. The venting ended in anger.

A few weeks later, my friend called cheery-voiced to say she had decided to start praying and reading the Book of Mormon again. She had never noticed the first fourteen chapters were all about the "goodness of God" until she started feeling it again. In February she and I launched a scripture expedition, searching for understanding of Christ's atonement. I wish I had space to write everything we found about God's grace and the changing power of his relentless love—his mercy. Paul captured our quest in one question: "Despisest thou the riches of his *goodness* and forbearance and longsuffering; knowing not that the *goodness of God* leadeth thee to repentance?" (Romans 2:4; emphasis added).

That year spring forgot to come in the outer world, but it arrived right on time in my friend's inner world. One March night, I was sitting alone in a meetinghouse—waiting. On my right was an open classroom door; on my left, a closed bishop's door. Beyond the open door, I heard a man explaining that we should be reluctant to talk about God's unconditional love for us. He feared that some people would think they can do anything they want to and God will still love them. In a clear inner voice, the Holy Ghost told me, "The man is

45

wrong. See what *only* God's unconditional love can do."
I looked to the left and then from behind the closed door, I
heard my friend and the members of the disciplinary council
laughing.

She had decided to go before a disciplinary council only
after she read Christ's promise to be her advocate. My friend,
the lawyer, needed a defender. Her remorse and humility
brought her the most powerful advocate in the universe: she
would not appear alone; if she would be honest, he and she
would "plead together" (Isaiah 43:26); he would put his
"strength" in her to "order [her] cause" and "fill [her] mouth"
(Job 23:4, 6); he would ask the Father to remember the death
of his sinless Son and reward her with everlasting life because
she believes in the Son (D&C 45:3–5); and the Father would
direct the disciplinary council's decision (D&C 58:20). The decision was simple and kind. All three council members said that
scriptures—recurring messages of God's unconditional love
and advocacy—were coursing through their minds the entire
day before they met.

Now my friend is in the temple, in her ward, and in God's
grace. If all-powerful God's redeeming and gracious love
should be his sole means of holding onto his children, why
should we weak mortals think control will ever do anything
but force them away?

Human control wounds and starves the soul. It damages
the human will to repent. Prolonged external control saps the
soul of its power and fills it with helplessness—the sense of not
really knowing or liking what one is doing but feeling compelled to do it anyway. Controlling and shaming are not God's
way to salvation. People cannot be shamed into spirituality;
they can be shamed only into shame.

Some people dominate their spouses or children by
demanding obedience to them in all things—even though,
unlike God, they can't see the future or alter it. But the domi-
neering, however well-meaning, don't stand for God—they try

to stand in front of him. They stunt the growth of a strong inner life in those who either submit to, or feel forced to rebel against, their control. Overcontrolled people seldom learn to feel God's power, guidance, approval, and pleasure inside themselves. Their battered conscience and inner life can die from disuse or distortion.

Lucifer is Satan because he wants to stand *between* God and us, because he wants to destroy moral agency, our power, by having all decisions made by forces *outside* us (see Moses 4:3). Jesus is Christ because he wants to stand *with* God and us, because he seeks to perfect moral agency by having all decisions made by choices *inside* us (see 2 Nephi 2:27). Moral agency is the soul of the Atonement, which promises God's life and mind to all those who choose them freely. Fortunately, we need not fear others' choices. Human attempts to grab power don't thwart God. If he can't work through people, he will work around them—even parents.

One of the most defining examples of the Lord's working around a parent he couldn't work through is that of Isaac being *forced* to pass on to Jacob the Abrahamic oath and covenant. During two face-to-face visits, the Lord had explained to Isaac that fulfillment of the oath and covenant meant continuation of a righteous, endless posterity (see Genesis 26:2–4, 24). The Lord even revealed to Rebekah that the younger twin would be the next patriarch (see Genesis 25:23–24), which she probably told Isaac. Yet, although Esau's hedonistic ways and pagan wives caused his parents "grief of mind" (Genesis 26:34, 35), Isaac was intent on giving Esau the Abrahamic oath and blessing. Esau, however, was in no condition to rear a righteous posterity, much less pass on God's power and priesthood. He had already violated the oath. The covenant would have died with him.

I used to wonder how the Lord could have approved of Rebekah's plan to trick her husband into blessing Jacob or of Jacob's outright lies to his blind, dying father. The past few years, however, I've wondered how Isaac could have so obdurately resisted foresight, common sense, personal revelation, and baseline tribal loyalty. He knew. He had had years of powerful enlightenment. He understood the import of the blessing. Yet he clung to a decision that would have altered Jacob's foreordained course of events, destroyed the house of Israel, and made prophecy a lie. Of course, that was not to be. Jacob's destiny was the world's destiny. The Lord had to work around Isaac until he could finally work through him—until Isaac's will matched the Lord's will.

I've known parents like Isaac, fundamentally good people who nonetheless insist on decisions that are contrary to the Lord's will for their children. Should the children be open to the Lord, their divinely mandated course of events moves forward anyway—often through other people the Lord sends their way. The parents merely suffer the pain of exclusion and miss the pleasure of participating in their children's growth.

The best way to stop blocking others' growth is to keep growing yourself. Growth means positive change.

More important than the inner power to *resist* external pressure is the inner power to *change* external circumstances. Father Lehi explained that we may act on the events of the insecure outer world rather than react to them (see 2 Nephi 2:11). Last year I started thinking about how the fallen, unchanged, natural mind is a natural enemy to just about everyone. So I decided to invite change in my mental habits by controlling the predatory little thoughts, comments, and actions that just seem to roll out—naturally, of course. But self-control was frustrating; I was just blocking expression. I needed new thoughts and feelings.

One day a prayer came into my mind and has stayed. When someone insults or irritates me, I find myself saying: "I do that, too. Heavenly Father, please forgive me as I forgive him or her." The result was amazing. I started experiencing on-the-spot healing and forgetting. Only after a few weeks of this prayer did I realize I was following the Lord's model (see Matthew 6:12).

I wish I could say I've become gracious. I have become less petty, and I'm now trying proactive grace. The other day I received some toxic E-mail from a woman who seems to enjoy sniping. Usually I sort through her spleen for her substance and then push *delete*. This time I replied immediately, thanking her for the information. After several hours, I received a reply: "You're welcome." Since then her E-mail has been at least civil if not kind. Maybe that's next. We all may nurture our soul by returning grace for spite.

Tender care of our inner lives causes us to be strong, mature, and active; injury or neglect of our inner lives causes us to be weak, immature, and passive. We constantly nurture our inner life through every truth told, prayer prayed, thought devoted, covenant kept, promise honored, tithe paid, sacrifice offered, scripture read, praise given, hand held, abuse withheld, service rendered, sin cleansed.

In the parable of the ten virgins, the five wise virgins could not give their oil—symbolic of the inner life—to the five foolish virgins, nor could the five foolish virgins receive it. Think of this parable in terms of family relations. Each family member can and ultimately must have her or his own inner relationship with the Father—separate from parents', spouse's, or anyone else's relationship. Spiritual power must be developed gradually and personally through a long-term, free-flowing relationship with the Father.

Sometimes parents may wonder if immature, controlling behavior has permanently ruined their important relationships and skewed their children's inner vision of God. The Atonement says no. The Atonement says, Give place for the Spirit and start to heal where you are now by letting Christ take you where he is. "No one can go back and make a brand-new start, my Friend. But anyone can start from here and make a brand-new end."[2]

49

Grace, power, mercy, and justice are not rewards God will hand out on Judgment Day to those who are strong enough to choose right until they become perfect. They are undeserved gifts for this moment without which we have little power of choice and no chance of perfection. It is useless to think, "I'll get myself straightened out and then God will bless me." Without God we have no power to straighten anything out. Holiness is not the way to Christ. Christ is the way to holiness.

Listen to God's promise of inner life to those who ask, yield, and trust: he will give "*exceedingly abundantly above* all that we *ask or think,* accordingly to the *power* that worketh in *us*" (Ephesians 3:20; emphasis added). "Let us therefore come boldly unto the throne of grace, that we may obtain mercy, and find grace to help in time of need" (Hebrews 4:16).

As Elder Merrill J. Bateman reminded us, the Atonement is not only *infinite* but *intimate*.[3] In Tennyson's words: "Closer is he than breathing and nearer than hands and feet."[4] And in the Lord's own words: "When thou passest through the waters, I will be with thee; . . . when thou walkest through the fire, thou shalt not be burned. . . . For I am the Lord thy God . . . thy Saviour. . . . Thou [art] precious in my sight. . . . Fear not: for I am with thee" (Isaiah 43:2–5).

NOTES

1. Corrie ten Boom, *The Hiding Place* (New York: Bantam Books, 1971), 195.

2. As quoted in *Bless Your Heart* (calendar), Series II (Edina, Minn.: Heartland Samples, 1990).

3. Merrill J. Bateman, "The Power to Heal from Within," *Ensign,* May 1994, 14.

4. Alfred, Lord Tennyson, *The Higher Pantheism* [1869], stanza 6.

RUSSIAN WOMEN: GAINING ROOTS, GROWING STRONG

DEIRDRE M. PAULSEN

> *So the mermaid she sang, filled with sadness and pain,*
> *With a sorrow she could not explain,*
> *And the stream leapt and danced and rushed noisily on,*
> *And the clouds in its depths whirled and spun.[1]*

These words of Russian poet Mikhail Lermontov express how I felt—the sorrow, the whirling confusion—saying good-bye at the end of my first trip to Russia in 1993. Galina Sysoeva, a Russian folklorist, my guide and friend, was one of a kaleidoscope of Russian women who touched me deeply.

Life is not now, nor has it ever been, easy for these extraordinary women, especially the grandmothers, or *babushkas,* as they are fondly called. Faced with the Bolshevik Revolution, World War I, Stalin's purges, husbands killed in the Great Patriotic War (World War II), forced starvation in the Ukraine, and meager, if any, pensions, these women have eked out an existence in a third-world country that we had assumed to be our equal. I found myself searching deeply within myself to match their wellsprings of humanity and love. Often I found myself lacking.

Deirdre Murray Paulsen teaches folklore classes at Brigham Young University in Salt Lake Center and serves as a writing consultant and the Writing Fellows Director at BYU. She and her husband, David Finn Paulsen, are the parents of five children. Deirdre and David teach the Young Single Adult Sunday School class in their stake.

As we parted, Galina gave me the beaded necklace she was wearing. Of her own making, the necklace could not be replaced because Russian glass beads are now unavailable in Russia. Deeply moved, I told my translator, Ilya, that I couldn't accept it. Ilya said to me, "When a Russian gives you something, it's from the heart and you must accept." I did, but what could I give in return? I wanted to give my heart, but the closest I could manage were the heart-shaped earrings I was wearing.

On that first visit, Galina invited me to return to Russia to lead a research expedition with her into the villages of southern Russia. If I could go back to see Galina's life work, perhaps the gift I could give her would be the technology to record Russian roots. I knew that Galina, with only pencil and paper, had already recorded more than five hundred songs. With the support of many people at Brigham Young University, I returned with a documentary crew in August 1994.

I had some apprehensions. Galina and I were unified by our common interest in Russian folklore, but how would Russian villagers treat our crew? We were their cold-war rivals, bringing American high technology into the villages. Would Russians resent us? Would they perform for us? Food was scarce. Would we starve? Where would we sleep?

Granola bars in hand, our group ventured into the remote villages in the Southern Black Earth region of Russia, where, we were told, no foreigners had ever set foot.[2] The Russians' generosity took us by surprise. In every village we were greeted with the same bread-and-salt ceremonies that Alexander Solzhenitsyn received on his return to Russia[3] and with banquets of food (even though the Russian farmers in this area had not been paid for seven months). Many greeted us with tears and memories of fighting side-by-side with Americans in World War II and joining with us in the victory celebrations after the Battle of the Elbe in Germany. They welcomed us with singing and dancing and with gifts from their walls and their tables. They gave up their beds for us.

Welcoming the visitor is a strong tradition throughout Russia. As Galina explained, "We have a saying—first, you bring a person into your home, feed him, give him something to drink, give him a bath, *then* you ask why he has come to see you." The villagers' welcome moved us deeply. "Thank you for coming to see us," one elderly *babushka* said. "We were preparing to die and you have revived us. Finally, something to celebrate!" Another woman volunteered, "We love you. You are such good people. Very good. Just like we are. Our entire world waited for you. We wondered what Americans would be like. And it turns out you are just like us."

Even though these women have suffered much more deprivation than we have, their hopes and dreams for a good family, for religious values, for good friends are the same as ours. And there is hope for these women. I found that already resilient Russian women are finding their lost roots under *perestroika* and growing stronger emotionally and spiritually, even as conditions in their country deteriorate further.

MYTHIC ROOTS: RUSSIA AS MOTHER

I had previously thought of Russia in terms of male figures: the Vikings who conquered in A.D. 860; Vladimir I who brought Christianity in A.D. 988; the Mongol khans, who ruled for 250 years; the Czars, especially Ivan the Terrible and Peter the Great; the Communist leaders—Lenin, Stalin, Brezhnev, Gorbachev, Yeltsin; soldiers marching in Red Square—a very masculine country. Oh, yes, there was Catherine the Great, but I considered her an anomaly.

Yet my experience with Russia was largely feminine. The mayors of the villages were female, the farmers in the countryside were female; in fact, the inhabitants of the villages were predominately female. I have since read that 80 percent of the doctors, 75 percent of teachers, and 82 percent of health care and other social service workers are women.[4] Women manage the money and the homes. But more than that, as I traveled

53

with Galina, I learned that women are the repositories of tradition and morals. It's the *babushkas* who are teaching their grandchildren to pray, to sing, and to dance the traditional rituals.

Kubaneva Nina Konstantinova, one of our Russian translators, explained the role of women in Russia: "A large number of men died in the war. . . . Therefore our women value men, spoil them. . . . The second generation of men after the war stopped considering themselves masculine, it seems to me. So women carry a lot of responsibility on their shoulders. They are the leaders here. They fulfill the largest role in the family. . . . Real men that take responsibility for women and their families are very hard to find in Russia."[5]

Even so, the strength of the Russian women surprised and puzzled me. How did they emerge from a Russia so long controlled by a strong male autocracy? I have since discovered that a Russian tradition of strong women predates the male autocracy. Written records and artifacts indicate that a female divinity was prominent until the twelfth century.[6]

The Matrioshka doll seems to be a carryover of this great divine female power, a symbol of Mother Russia. Joanna Hubbs, author of *Mother Russia,* asks, "Who is not familiar with the round and brightly colored Matrioshka doll? She is the most common of all Russian toys. . . . Broken apart at the stomach, she spills out many identical dolls, one inside the other in descending order, until the tiny center doll appears as though it were her youngest. One containing many, she seems ever-fertile."[7]

Hubbs feels that "more than a doll and a relic from a forgotten past, Matrioshka remains a symbolic embodiment of 'Mother Russia'. Just as the doll is to be found everywhere, . . . the habit of mind which sees the mother as the 'nest' where her children can find refuge and identity remains strong." During my visit, I noted this attachment of the Russians to the country as mother. The land and physical features, even cities, are given "maternal epithets." Huge rivers, for example, are called Matushka Volga or "Little Mother Volga." Mother Kiev is "the city which is popularly called the birth giver," and Mother Moscow "nourished Russia's growth and is identified with her heart."[8]

Russians give the earth strong motherly attributes. "In the peasant tradition," says Hubbs, "the soil is sacred: The peasants implore 'Mother Moist Earth' for aid in their lives."[9] Galina told me that her folk group, *Lada*, performed at Chernobyl eight weeks after the meltdown of the nuclear reactor. Horrified, I asked if they'd worn protective clothing, and of course they hadn't. But Galina reassured me. She'd known they weren't in danger, she said, because she smelled the earth and it smelled fine, and she tasted it and it tasted fine. Needless to say, I was not much reassured, but this incident illustrates the Russian trust in "Mother Moist Earth"—trust that she will sustain them and won't be defiled. In fact, until the early 1900s, peasants would "swallow a mouthful of earth" to seal their oaths, much as we would place our hand on the Bible.[10] Couples during the same period ate earth to "confirm their union."[11]

In Russia, respect for Mother Earth extends to respect for all motherhood. The Russians I met accorded me, as a mother of five children, incredible reverence. They would touch me with awe and say, "You are the mother of five children. You are so blessed." These women who had a strong sense of motherhood and a centuries-rooted desire for many children, had few children and repeated abortions so they could meet their heavy, state-mandated work quotas.[12] When they found out that the Communist state couldn't fulfill its promises, they were far past their childbearing years. They had been duped and felt tremendously cheated.

Yet despite their losses, there was something subconscious, almost mystical, giving these women strength. I now believe the centuries-old Russian myths and folklore, suppressed but not obliterated under Communism, strengthen the Russian woman's view of herself as mother and provider.

GENEALOGICAL ROOTS

A second change to enter the women's lives under *perestroika* has been the ability to obtain their genealogy. It is one of the great ironies of Russia that the country with one of the longest unbroken chains of traditions allowed Communism to erase that memory. For at least a thousand years, cultural history remained almost unchanged in Russia. The wedding ceremonies, games, songs, musical accompaniment, foods, family organization, and religious beliefs go back to A.D. 1000 and beyond. But the Bolshevik Revolution in 1917 changed all that. Communists not only disrupted the customs and beliefs but forbade memory. That devastated a culture with deep roots in its past and a strong, central family organization that revered its ancestry.

Igor V. Sakharov, president of the recently founded Russian Genealogical Society in Saint Petersburg, told us that "the Communist regime wanted to eliminate memory because memory was dangerous for the regime. If you had a rich grandmother or grandfather, or priests, or officers of the Czar's army, or just an educated person in your family tree, that was a reason for discrimination and repression. So everybody tried to hide their own past." Old personal documents and letters were burned, portraits and photographs destroyed, family relics hidden, and surnames even changed to obliterate family connections. "That is why most Russians now do not know anything about their family roots and do not even understand that there could have been anything interesting to know."

Sakharov remembers: "Sometimes, [the government] would eliminate an entire mass of documents." Many people destroyed their personal archives: "In this manner there was a massive elimination of documented memories. . . . Never have so many people disappeared, because you can kill people by forgetting them. To forget a person is to destroy a person. . . . The result is that people are left without roots. A person without roots isn't complete. He's somewhat ill and maybe even very ill." Sakharov worries that Russia is now "facing a profound cultural, intellectual, moral, and spiritual rupture, a gap between modern generations and the generations of our fathers. The people were cut off from their roots. We now observe in Russia a loss of historical memory, a disease which can be called historical amnesia."[13]

As Sakharov noted, most people in Russia think they are descended from peasants, because under Communism that was the only safe group to be related to. Since *perestroika,* however, many have found out that they are really descended from nobility, the intellectual class, or from clerics. A case in point is Nina Bazarskaya, a professor at the Institute of Forestry in Voronezh. Nina's grandfather on her father's side joined the Russian Orthodox clergy when he was in his thirties to protest atrocities against the church. In the 1930s, under Stalin's regime, he and his uncles and his great-grandfather, who was in his nineties, were exiled to northern Siberia, where they all died.

Nina's father was seventeen when his father was imprisoned, and the experience affected the rest of his life. He became a forester so he didn't have to fill out a lot of official forms and for half the year could be in the forest where no one cared about his origins. He never, ever talked about his father, and Nina wondered why. Only recently her father showed her the last letter her grandfather had written from the camps before he died. It was a "great psychological shock to read a letter from a man who was doomed to death just because he was a priest in the Russian Orthodox faith," says Nina. Yet learning of her progenitors filled her with pride and with a great feeling of completeness.[14]

Valentin Rasputin, one of Russia's finest writers of the post-Stalinist period, wrote: "Truth is in memory. The person without memory is without life."[15] Russians are slowly having their memories and their lives restored. This memory is giving them tremendous strength—strength they very much need to deal with the political and economic hardships in Russia. Finally they are gaining a sense of connectedness.

FOLK ROOTS

The revival of folk and religious customs is also bringing new meaning to Russian women's lives. Many women in their seventies, eighties, and nineties are finally free to share their historical past and collective memory now that the Iron Curtain has fallen. In fourteen small villages throughout rural Russia, we recorded these *babushkas* as they struggled to recall exactly how a ritual used to be performed and how a song was sung. This was their way of resurrecting the Russian soul.

From Galina I knew that folk traditions still existed but that the Communist regime had forbidden their practice. Communist leaders despised traditions and rituals, which they felt linked people to a past of prejudice and superstition—a burden to a new society. So I was amazed to see how many traditional songs had been preserved; how many dances were still being danced; how many hundred-year-old costumes had been carefully tucked away; and how many festive rituals had been continually performed in secret.

Villager Natalia Chertova says, "These songs purify the Russian soul. There are happy songs, sad songs, spiritual songs. . . . When you sing an old song your soul is resurrected." To explain this resurgence of traditional folklore, Galina uses the metaphor of a tree, which was cut down, its roots covered by asphalt. The Russian soul was never killed, she insists. The roots were simply covered by the asphalt of Communism: "Where traditions are strong, they give new sprout."

Accustomed to the pseudofolklore promoted under the Soviets, even Galina hadn't known much about what she now identifies as "authentic folklore." In 1987 she visited the rural villages to learn songs to teach her choir in Voronezh, one of the larger cities in Russia, but "what they sang in the villages and what they sang on the [city] stage were completely different art forms."

Since then, Galina has devoted her life and her family's sparse finances to the preservation of "authentic culture," including buying old costumes and establishing a private museum, perhaps the only one in Russia, so that her fellow Russians can rediscover their roots. She and her husband had been saving for five years to buy a television, when she came upon some very old regional costumes. When she told her husband, he urged her, "Take the money and buy the costumes. . . . A TV we'll buy in five years. . . . A TV doesn't have any value. It's a diversion." Galina feels the urgency of her mission: "These carriers of folklore—they are dying. In another five years or so, these people will be gone."

On our visits I was especially impressed by the villagers' houses. Inside and out, they were painted bright colors with fanciful designs, such as snowmen or flowers. Their ancestors had embroidered nature symbols on the sleeves of their costumes to protect the wearers from evil. These same symbols were on the linen towels they draped around their icons and family pictures. Their beds were high off the ground, often curtained, and always had two huge, heavily embroidered pillows. (We never did figure out how to sleep on the pillows.)

We were humbled to learn that the villagers had anticipated the visit of "rich Americans" with embarrassment, thinking we would look down on their homes and their villages and their lives. Far from it. We agreed with Galina: "They [the villagers] are an amazing example of how to live beautifully. Even under difficult conditions, they don't wait for someone to make their world beautiful. They do it themselves."

RELIGIOUS ROOTS

For older Russians, reestablishing roots means a return to Russian Orthodoxy—rebuilding the Russian Orthodox churches, finding the icons or painting new ones, teaching the grandchildren the tenets of the faith. In the area we visited, old maps attest to the density of churches whose onion domes used to sparkle along the Don River. Galina explains, "To conquer faith . . . [the Communists] destroyed churches, which were at the center of our culture." So for Galina Sysoeva and most Russians, a search for spiritual as well as cultural roots includes returning to the Orthodox faith.

Knowing her concerns, I asked Galina if she resented other religions coming which threatened traditional ways. "I have thought a lot about that question," she answered. "At first it did bother me. And I still think that for the older people, you can't separate their souls, the Russian soul, from the Orthodox church. But for the younger people, who have had spiritual and moral values torn away from them by the state, any religion is a blessing, and so, for them, I welcome new religions."

The Church of Jesus Christ of Latter-day Saints is one of the "new" religions that has recently begun proselyting in Russia. Latter-day Saint missionaries entered Russia from Finland in 1989. Today there are six missions, a dramatic growth of the Church. What kind of people are joining the LDS Church in Russia? They are strong and dedicated, and many have struggled because Russian Orthodoxy and Russia are so closely linked. For every Russian, "to change religion is a great process, a very difficult process, the process of moral torture," said Professor Nina Bazarskaya, the first Latter-day Saint convert in Voronezh. "You need to think it over, again and again, to think if you're doing right."

Nina first learned of the Church through Trevor McKee, a BYU professor whom she met at a conference near Moscow and invited to lecture in Voronezh. She took him to the Easter ceremony, the greatest festival in the Russian Orthodox Church.

"Even though the lights, the music, the golden robes were wonderful," she says, "I couldn't feel the Spirit." The BYU professor encouraged her to attend an LDS church meeting held by students he had brought with him to teach English to Russian preschoolers. Nina records: "When I came to this meeting, the moment I entered the room, I felt the Spirit. This to me was my personal revelation."

Feeling, however, as if she were betraying her grandfather who had died in exile in Siberia for his Russian Orthodox beliefs, Nina went to the country for three days and prayed. Finally, she received assurance that her relatives were loyal to the only truth they had at the time, but that she needn't feel guilty for leaving the Russian Orthodox faith in searching for greater truth. It was a confirmation she desperately needed before she could join the LDS Church.[16]

Larissa Kolotneva, a young LDS Russian student who translated for us, recently sent me her testimony. "Now I am a seminary teacher and I am so very happy! I read the scriptures every day and I thank my Heavenly Father for talking to me. The Gospel is very simple: Seek pure things and you will be happy. Things we cannot do, the Lord will do for us if we stay worthy. I know that."[17] Larissa closes our last correspondence with, "I love you very much and all my brothers and sisters in the gospel all over the world."

I love these wonderfully warm and strong Russian women who are relishing discovering their roots. Erasing "historical amnesia" is not easy—it has been a painful yet jubilant process of Russians merging recollections to achieve a collective memory.

NOTES

Nina Bzarskaya will be a plenary speaker at the 1996 Women's Conference at BYU.

Galina Sysoeva and fifteen of her students from the Voronezh Institute of Art have formed a group called "Volya" or "Freedom." They have been invited by the Springville Folkfest (Springville, Utah) and the Red Butte Gardens (Salt Lake City, Utah) to perform July 1997.

1. Mikhail Lermontov, "The Mermaid," *Selected Works* (Moscow: Progress Publishers, 1978), 29.

2. The team had different responsibilities: Dale Cressman was documentary producer; Roger Gunn, production manager; Jennifer Lloyd, Russian culture consultant and translator; Sam Prigg, head videographer; Steve Kingsolver, assistant videographer; Deirdre Paulsen, folklore consultant. Our expedition was funded by the BYU film committee, the College of Fine Arts and Communications, and KBYU. The resulting documentary, "Hidden Memory," first aired on KBYU December 1995.

3. The bread-and-salt ceremony is the traditional Russian way to welcome foreigners. In our case, ten to fifteen villagers in peasant costumes met our bus as we entered every village. They sang and offered us flowers. One of the villagers prominently carried an elaborately decorated round loaf of bread on a long, embroidered "towel." I was expected to break off a chunk of this thick-crusted bread and dip it into a small glass containing salt, which perched on top of the bread. The other members of our team then did the same. This ceremony symbolizes hospitality. By offering bread (the staple of life) and salt (long a luxury item), the Russians offered us their finest, assuring us that we would never go hungry while we stayed with them.

4. Novosti Press Agency, *Yearbook USSR '87* (Moscow, 1987), 163, 167, quoted in Barbara Evans Clements "Later Development," *Russia's Women: Accommodations, Resistance, Transformation,* ed. Clements et al. (Los Angeles: University of California Press, 1991), 274.

5. Kubaneva Nina Konstantinova, interview with the author, Voronezh, Russia, August 1994.

6. Joanna Hubbs, *Mother Russia: Feminine Myth in Russian Culture* (Bloomington: Indiana University Press, 1988), 11–12.

7. Hubbs, xi.

8. Hubbs, xii-xiii.

9. Hubbs, xiii-xiv.

10. Linda J. Ivanits, *Russian Folk Belief* (New York: M. E. Sharpe, Inc., 1989), 15.

11. Olga Semyonova Tian Shanskaia, *Village Life in Late Tsarist Russia,* trans. and ed. David L. Ransel (Bloomington: Indiana University Press, 1993), 167.

12. Neither the Communist state nor the Russian government has ever restricted family size as has, for example, China. On the contrary, the government has tried to ban abortion in an effort to increase family size. There is a continuing concern in Russia about declining population. So why did the peasant

women I interviewed have few children? Susan Bridger in her 1983 article "Soviet Rural Women: Employment and Family Life," reprinted in *Russian Peasant Women,* ed. Beatrice Farnsworth and Lynne Viola (New York: Oxford University Press, 1992), 289, explains this seeming contradiction: "In its anxiety to raise the birthrate, the state is putting pressure on women with heavy commitments at work and in the home to have more children. At the same time, little effort is being made to challenge the apathy and inertia of men within the family. Inevitably, many women clearly resent the burdens placed upon them and see the restriction of their family size as the only way to obtain a manageable workload."

13. Igor V. Sakharov, interview with Jennifer Lloyd, Saint Petersburg, Russia, August 1994.

14. Nina Bazarskaya, interview with author, Voronezh, Russia, August 1994.

15. Valentin Rasputin, *Farewell to Matyora* (Evanston, Ill.: Northwestern University Press, 1991), 181.

16. Nina Bazarskaya, interview with author, Salt Lake City, Utah, July 1994.

17. Larissa Kolotneva has been called to be the Relief Society president of the Voronezh Branch in Russia. She has applied to do graduate work in linguistics at BYU in 1996–97.

1948

ELAINE W. CHRISTENSEN

She was learning German that year,
a war bride, living in Darmstadt,
trying to say *ich* in the back of her throat,
the guttural *r* of *Herr* and *Frau,* to introduce
herself and her lieutenant husband,
pursing her lips
to form the strange vowel sounds
of *umlaut u* and *o,*
the difficult blends
of *pf* in *Apfel* and *zw* in *zwei.*

Years later, when I studied German,
these sounds surprised me, shaping
themselves on my tongue as easily
as a baby finds its fist and sucks.

That spring she sat long hours at the piano,
exercising her fingers
with Hanon first, then Mozart.
When each finger knew its strength,
she played Chopin. When her hands
reached the octave with ease,
Beethoven followed. Closing her music
and her eyes, she'd finish

Elaine W. Christensen, recipient of the Utah Poet of the Year award in 1990 for her book *At the Edges,* received her bachelor's degree from Utah State University in German and English. She and her husband, Roger P. Christensen, have five children. Elaine teaches Gospel Doctrine in her ward and is an institute instructor at Salt Lake Community College.

with Rachmaninoff, each finger an emotion,
each key its release.

> The fortes, the pianissimos,
> each rallentando pulsed in me
> and I knew before I was born
> I would hunger, I would hate,
> I would fear, I would seek sorrow.

That summer as August approached
and she grew awkward, swelling
with the heat,
my mother stood evenings at the window
wishing some breath of the river
might move in the heavy draperies,
might ease her longing for blue mountains,
for arched skies of home.
Here the sky spread like a flat sheet
from one corner of the horizon
to the other.
She wished for blue, anything blue.
She said my eyes were her wish granted.

> When I saw her mountains, the sky,
> chips of blue glass in every window,
> I cried.
> I knew this was home,
> like an infant knows,
> still slick and bloody,
> to turn its head toward the sound
> of its mother's voice.

SEEKING THE WILL OF GOD: BIT BY BIT BY BIT

PAM KAZMAIER

When I was asked to discuss seeking God's will in decision making, I was sure I should say no. I had just been watching the news on CNN, and interest rates and the stock market were falling. My husband and I had prayerfully invested five thousand dollars in the stock that was plummeting. Obviously, I'm not a good decision maker, I thought. I was waiting for an opening in the conversation so I could say no. Then my knees started shaking just as they do before I bear my testimony on fast Sunday at church. I felt I was supposed to say yes—that I was supposed to tell of my recent experience in making the hardest decision of my life: I quit my career as a nurse to stay at home with my two small children.

Please understand, I'm not advocating that all women should quit their jobs to stay home with their children— especially after having done it for two years. I thought I worked hard as a nurse—but being a mother is the hardest thing I've ever done.

Let me explain why this decision was so difficult. I grew up in Illinois. I was completely ignorant about Latter-day Saints. I thought they all wore black and lived in the Rocky Mountains.

Pam Kazmaier enjoyed hospital nursing for twenty years. Now she and her husband, Kevin Craig Kazmaier, are the parents of two active boys. Pam teaches an even more active Sunbeam class in her ward.

I was reared by a mother who was a feminist back in the fifties before that term was coined. She reared my two sisters and me not to marry or have children but to get an education and have a career. My father did not disagree.

At the age of eighteen, I entered a convent, largely because I didn't want to worry about being married and having children. I valued my mother's teachings and was afraid that if I went to college, I'd fall in love, get married, and have children. A convent seemed a good place to avoid all that.

The scriptures are another strong reason I entered the convent; they are also the reason I left. The longer I was in the convent, the more I read the scriptures and prayed, the more I felt the Holy Spirit tell me that I was in the wrong place. I didn't understand that then. I do now. I *was* in the wrong place there; I was supposed to be here.

So even though being a nun was a wonderful part of my life, after four years, I left the convent. Making that decision was very tough. I had never taken my commitment lightly. While I was a nun, I began nurse's training in earnest. I loved nursing—and I am not talking about breast-feeding. To tell the truth, I do not do nursing babies well, but I was a great nurse. I loved the nursing profession and thought I would never leave it. I started at fourteen as a candy striper and completed my training in 1977 after I had left the convent.

I was not like young Latter-day Saint women who are taught eternal values early and are groomed to marry in the temple and be wives and mothers. Those were all foreign ideas to me. But at twenty-eight I did marry. Like me, my husband Kevin supported the idea of women working and believed they should be independent. At the time of our marriage, Kevin and I decided not to have children because they'd get in the way of our work. His career came first; my career came first. It was a great match. To you, career first, family second sounds very foreign, but to us in the world, that attitude was very common.

I loved everything about the hospital—the smell, the excitement. It was just a great place; it felt like home. I joined the Church because of people I met there. I found myself taking care of patients who were different from anybody I had ever met. They were amazing; I wanted to be like them. These patients had something I didn't have—peace. I was attracted to their strength in crisis, their family unity. They were mannerly and polite, well-groomed and refined. To me, my conversion experience was a miracle. I joined the Church in Mesa, Arizona, and my life changed.

My patriarchal blessing said, "There are spirits reserved in the heavens so that you and your husband can have children." I thought, Yeah, right. These Mormons have all these children. Not me. Then, a year and a half later, my husband joined the Church, and his patriarchal blessing said, "There are *still* spirits reserved in heaven so that you and your wife can have children." "Oh, Kevin," I said, "I think we've got to have these children. Oh no." And so we did. We sold our Corvette and bought a family car. And here we are. At thirty-five I had my first little boy, and then at thirty-seven I had another.

I still never considered quitting work, though. I thought having the children was going to be enough. Then I had a run-in with a little pink pamphlet—*Mothers of Zion*. I hear it made quite a stir in the Church when it came out, but it didn't faze me because I didn't have any children then. When I first saw it, I thought, Oh yeah, right, uh-huh, very good, and I shelved it. It wasn't about me. But then one day my husband said, seeing me wrestle with motherhood and work, "Maybe you ought to think about quitting work." Ha! Quit work? He could just as well have said, "Maybe you ought to cut off your legs." I loved my job—and I was very good at it. I couldn't cook. I couldn't sew. I can't sing. I can't do anything. But give me a chest pain, and I know what to do.

I told my husband I would pray about quitting work, fully thinking the Lord would say, "Of course you can't quit your job. It's a vocation; it's a calling. You and I have done this for twenty years. You can't quit. People are waiting for you in the hospital." So I just prayed, "Okay, Lord, this is what Kevin thinks, but you and I both know . . ." and then on like that. I got up from my knees and never thought another thing about it. Here's the lesson: When you wrestle with questions like, Should I marry him/Should I not marry him? Should I move? Should I go back to school? remember this. When I have been about to go down the wrong path and take others with me, the Lord has intervened if I have stayed close to him.

The next day, this pink pamphlet that had been shelved for four years was hanging out of my bookshelves. My husband doesn't get up in my bookshelves. My kids were too little. And I hadn't been in that section—that was the dusty section. But the pink pamphlet was hanging out. That's the miracle. How did that happen? I had ten minutes before I left for work—I was never late for work—so I thought, Okay, I've got ten minutes to read this thing. There is something in here about mothers working. (That's how much attention I had paid to it when I first got it.) I thought, I'm going to read something in here that will prove to Kevin that I should keep on working. So I started reading the pamphlet, and before I knew it I was crying. I read, "No more sacred word exists in secular or holy writ than that of *mother*. There is no more noble work than that of a good and God-fearing mother."[1] It went on and on—"a mother's role is God-ordained." Oh, brother! I thought. I'm sunk. I cried all the way to work.

I had great babysitters. My kids were in better hands with them than they were with me. The sitters had play dough and children's tapes and other kids running around, and everybody was happy. I left our children with the babysitter on the way to work and said, "Yes! I'm out of here. I'm going someplace where I know what I'm doing." But this day I drove to work sobbing.

I'm not like Abraham, who could immediately sacrifice

Isaac the very next morning. I couldn't tell my head nurse, "I read this article and . . ." It took weeks and weeks, months and months. It was a very gradual change for me. I got home that night and thought, Sure, women are supposed to leave working at McDonald's and the dry cleaners, but I have this important calling of the Lord to be a nurse. So I checked in with the pamphlet again, only to read, "Finally President Kimball counsels, 'I beg of you, you who could and should be bearing and rearing a family: wives come home from the typewriter, the laundry, *the nursing* [emphasis added].'" I was devastated, shattered.

I began to pray with real intent this time. For months I prayed about it. I was on my knees to the Lord saying, "Lord, how can you expect me to give up something I am so good at to do something I am so bad at?" It didn't make any sense to me. And I heard the voice of the Lord: "I am just asking you to do something *else* now." I was speechless. I knew it was the voice of the Lord. It was that still, small voice I had read about in the scriptures. I thought, Oh, he wants me to do something *else* now. It isn't like he didn't appreciate all those years of service. He's asking me to do something *else* now.

I pondered that. That month I taught a Relief Society lesson in my ward and found a quotation from Harold B. Lee in the lesson materials that really helped. It began, "You may not like what comes from the authority of the Church."[2] Well, thank you for giving me at least *that* permission, I thought. Yes, I don't like what has come from the authority of the Church. "It may contradict your political views." I'm a member of NOW, the National Organization of Women, and yes, this contradicts my political views. "It may contradict your social views. It may interfere with some of your social life." No kidding. Stuck home with two little kids, my husband's gone half the time, all my friends are at work. The hospital *is* my social life. Then President Lee goes on to say, "But if you listen to these things, as if from the mouth of the Lord himself, with patience and faith . . . " In other words, I didn't have to do it right away. I was so glad he let me wean myself from full time, to part time, to on call. That is how my testimony has grown—bit by bit by bit.

The final step came for me one night when I came home after only four hours at the hospital. I drove into my driveway and saw my husband, my dear husband whom I love, outside speaking to our next-door neighbor. It was dark and cold. It gets that way in Arizona in the evenings even though it's hot during the days. There were my two little boys, barefoot and dirty. In wet T-shirts with their hair all caked, they looked like orphans. I just left four hours ago, I thought. How can they look this bad already? When I'm home I line those kids up just like my IV fluids. I organize them, and they are in bed and asleep by eight o'clock. They would have had their little jammies on and their baths and their prayers and their stories and their teethies brushed and everything.

It was not the moment to discuss with Kevin the differences in our parenting styles. So I went into the house, put down my stethoscope, rolled up my sleeves, and tore into the disaster area that used to be the kitchen. And I once again heard the calm voice, not my own, say in my mind, "There are others who can take your place at work, but there is no one who can take your place here." And I said, "No kidding!" Just like that. Out loud. I wasn't feeling at all spiritual at the time, so when I heard the voice of the Lord, I just said, "No kidding! No kidding."

As I said, I am no Abraham. Months had gone by since I had begun praying about work. It wasn't until the next week that I woke up one morning with the thought, I'm going to quit my job today. I need to tell Kevin. One day each week Kevin takes the kids to the sitter, and we spend the whole day together—we have lunch, go to a movie, even have an uninterrupted conversation. "Kevin," I said on this particular morning, "when you come back from taking the kids, I've got

71

something to tell you." He didn't know that I'd been brooding about work for months and months.

Kevin was my last hurdle. He really liked my salary, really liked the fact that I was working. If there was some way I could convince him . . . I was on my knees in prayer right there by the bathtub after he left, praying, "Heavenly Father, I've got to quit today, and I don't know how to do it. I don't know how I'm going to tell Kevin, and you've got to help me."

When Kevin came home, I was sobbing. I felt like somebody had died. Kevin came in and said, "The Holy Spirit told me on the way home in the truck. You're going to quit your job today." I was so grateful to Heavenly Father for hearing my prayer so I didn't have to tell Kevin. I nodded and cried some more, and Kevin said, "It's okay. Let 'em go pound sand." I don't know what that means, but those were his words.

"How do I do this?" I asked. "I've never quit a job. I've been there at this hospital for eleven years. I love nursing. Over twenty years I've been a nurse. I don't know how to do this."

"Well, you need to go tell your head nurse."

"Yeah. Go tell the head nurse. Okay." So we got in the car and drove to the hospital. I sobbed all the way up the stairs to the sixth floor. I didn't even care who saw me. I couldn't stop crying. Doctors and patients wondered what in the world was wrong. Thank goodness my head nurse was in her office. I blurted out, "Sally, I've got to quit my job." And then she was crying and I was crying, and it was awful, just awful. But I did it. That was two years ago this week, and I am still alive.

I wish I could stand before you and say, "I just love the little ones—they're five and three now. I just love their laundry and the peanut butter and the spilled popsicles. I'm just having so much fun with my children." I really am not having fun.

What I miss most are the angels singing for me at the end of my shift. Many times when something critical happened during my shift, like a patient hemorrhaging or a difficult delivery, when I walked out to the car after work about one o'clock in the morning, I could hear the angels sing for me. I felt they were grateful. They applauded for how I had helped. These past two years I haven't heard them sing for me one time. But I know that twenty years from now they're going to sing for me again. I know they will.

And I know I am doing the right thing now, too. At times, even with very little children, you can actually get a conversation of some sort going or experience some kind of spiritual feeling with them. When that happens, I'll look at my watch and realize, I would have been counting narcotics. I would have missed this. It's not just my body that's at home now; my mind is there, too. Even when I was working part time or on call, my mind was at the hospital. I'd call the hospital, "You want me to come in? How's it going?" Because I am home day in and day out now, answering questions and being there for them, I know my children have a peace in their lives that wasn't there before.

In Matthew 6:33, the Savior instructs: "Seek ye first the kingdom of God, and his righteousness; and all these things shall be added unto you." If he had not said "first," wouldn't that be easier? Wouldn't it be great if he'd said, "Seek ye *third* the kingdom of God"? Wouldn't that be a lot more convenient? But he says, "Seek ye *first* the kingdom of God." Seeking the kingdom of God first is *hard*. Usually I find I have to sacrifice something of the world to do it. Right now, that means putting my ambitions aside for my children.

NOTES

1. Ezra Taft Benson, "To the Mothers in Zion," Parents Fireside, Salt Lake City, Utah, 22 Feb. 1987; see Ezra Taft Benson, *Come Listen to a Prophet's Voice* (Salt Lake City: Deseret Book, 1990), 25, 26.

2. Harold B. Lee, in "Be Not of the World," *Learn of Me: Relief Society Personal Study Guide 2* (Salt Lake City: The Church of Jesus Christ of Latter-day Saints, 1990), 23.

"BE A SPECIALIST YOURSELF IN THE TRUTH"

NANCY ROLLINS AHLANDER

As a young mother, I spent considerable effort and energy seeking out good books about parenting and family relations. In fact, one day one of my children, himself a great reader of *Little House* books, commented, "Mother, why don't you read something you enjoy?" I answered, "But I do enjoy this." I'm that kind of seeker; I enjoy learning—even without suspense, a good plot, exotic settings, or dashing characters. When my children were older, I worked my way, a few college credit hours at a time, toward a master's degree. I entered the halls of academia thinking, Now I'm going to find truth. I'm going to sort through theories with the pros.

My initial excitement soon waned. Each theory I encountered in my first two classes seemed to have some truth, much obvious untruth, and some ideas I could not sort into either camp. In learning about the authors of various theories, I was disheartened to discover that many of them led lives counter not only to gospel teaching but seemingly to their own theories as well. How could I give credence to their theories?

I asked a Latter-day Saint faculty member, counselor, and friend to help me sort things out from an LDS perspective.

Nancy Rollins Ahlander has a Ph.D. in family studies from Brigham Young University and is on the family science faculty at Ricks College. The mother of seven children, she teaches Home and Family Education in her ward Relief Society.

Although my friend was warm and empathetic, his response did not give me peace. I was searching for the true theory, the one that fit LDS beliefs; he insisted there was no such thing. In fact, LDS counselors could and did practice from any and all the various theories.

Compounding my frustration that semester, my skills lab teacher strongly advocated a theory I didn't like. Although the intent of the lab class was to experience a variety of counseling methods, she imposed her preferences, perhaps innocently, on the class. She believed a counselor should never self-disclose. But doesn't self-disclosure—sharing part of myself—help people open up to me? I wondered. She also denounced touching, hugging, and a nurturing stance as "infantilizing" and never appropriate in a counseling situation. But weren't there appropriate occasions when warmth and a hug might help others feel valued and trusted?

That semester was excruciating. Not only did I not find an indisputably true theory in theory class, but the one I had formed for myself was being crucified in skills lab. I felt as if I were sitting on a three-legged stool, with first one leg and then another being systematically kicked out from under me. My continuing studies eventually helped me replace the legs on my tottering stool.

First, I learned that experts disagree with each other. For nearly every person with scholarly credentials who takes a strong position on a certain subject, another with equally impressive scholarly credentials takes the opposite position on the very same issue. In fact, Neal Postman, a scholar in the field of education, has confessed that he and his coauthor and friend are often tempted, on finishing a book, to add as the last line "And vice versa!" They know that they could make a strong scholarly case for the opposing view as well.

Consider the current debates on family change as an example. With more teenage pregnancies, unwed mothers, divorce, single-parent families, stepfamilies, cohabitation, and same-sex partners, nobody questions that the family is changing. The disagreement centers on whether the changes signal family decline or simply family change, perhaps even an improvement allowing for more diversity and tolerance. Scholars studying families occupy every position on the continuum from those who predict disaster unless trends are reversed to those who celebrate the family's demise, bidding good riddance to an institution that was always oppressive to women and children anyway. More moderate positions range everywhere in between. Learning that even experts disagree and that a scholarly, well-reasoned case can be made for just about any position was a valuable lesson for me.

Second, in the course of my studies, I also discovered that scholars and experts change their minds. In fact, over the course of their careers, they may change their minds several times and in radical ways. For example, Jay Belsky, a brilliant child development scholar, early in his career championed the mainstream view that day care not only does not harm, but in some cases helps a child. Later in his career, after reviewing all the available research and conducting some of his own, Dr. Belsky published his new, politically unpopular opinion. In essence, his analysis showed that children under the age of one year who are in day care for more than twenty hours a week are at risk for a variety of negative effects. Scholars, especially intellectually honest scholars, change their minds.

This brings me to my third discovery. Research scholars ask questions based on fundamental assumptions. For example, a researcher would never ask, "How long does it take to teach a cow to talk?" or "How much fertilizer is needed to promote rock growth?" A fundamental assumption that cows don't talk and rocks don't grow eliminates those questions. But not all assumptions are as universally held or based on apparent realities like those are. For instance, if you assume that humans evolved from lower species, you ask different research questions from those you ask if you believe that humans had a premortal existence and are children of God. A scholar's assumptions shape both the questions asked and the interpretation of research findings. For instance, teenage pregnancies are increasing. So are sex education programs in schools. The assumptions some scholars bring to their research may lead them to believe that inadequate sex education in the schools has contributed to the problem of teenage pregnancy. Another set of assumptions could draw an alternate inference, however, that earlier and earlier exposure to sexual information without a moral context gives rise to the problem.

For me, these few examples of conflicting opinions illustrate not the uselessness of parenting books and resources or the foolishness of social science, my chosen field, but rather how knowing a little about the process of scholarship can help us in the search for truth and in our desire to be the best possible parent or grandparent.

Joseph F. Smith has advised: "Let love and peace, and the spirit of the Lord, kindness, charity, sacrifice for others, abound in your families. Banish harsh words, envyings, hatreds, evil speaking, obscene language and innuendo, blasphemy, and let the Spirit of God take possession of your hearts. Teach to your children these things, in spirit and power, sustained and strengthened by personal practice. Let them see that you are earnest, and practice what you preach. Do not let your children out to specialists in these things, but teach them by your own precept and example, by your own fireside. Be a specialist yourself in the truth."[1] In that spirit, let me share with you some of the questions I have learned to ask as I read expert parenting advice to keep me from being "tossed to and fro, and carried about with every wind of doctrine" (Ephesians 4:14).

First and foremost, I consciously impose my LDS assumptions as I evaluate expert advice. I ask, Is this in harmony with gospel principles? For example, most marriage and family college textbooks advise young people to experiment with several different lifestyle options, including cohabitation and same-sex unions, as preparation for marriage. When expert advice so blatantly opposes gospel principles, I take comfort in the words of Elder Rex D. Pinegar spoken to a group of LDS counselors: "Everything that came to me I had to measure against the gospel of Jesus Christ, and if it didn't fit, then I had two choices—I could put it into one of two categories, the discarded category or the set-it-over-here category, because I may not quite have been able to understand yet. But I did not adopt it until after I found out where it fit, and if it didn't fit, I found myself absolutely free to discard it."[2] So I ask myself, Does this advice invite me to do good, to deal justly, to walk uprightly? (see D&C 11:12).

Answering that question is fairly easy. A little tougher question is, What assumptions is this author making about human growth and development, or the nature of human relations, that allow him or her to make these recommendations or draw these conclusions? Some authors outline their underlying, fundamental assumptions in a preface; they want you to know up front where they're coming from. Others don't tell you. You may have to note patterns in their ideas or read between the lines. To help me do that, I ask myself, How else can I interpret this? and What does someone else say about this? I read other scholars. I ask other people's opinions. And I cultivate a healthy skepticism about statistics: As a friend once warned me, "Torture numbers long enough, and they'll confess to anything you want to hear."

Many years ago, I was part of a neighborhood book club. At one meeting, the younger mothers were almost in tears over a parenting book we had chosen to read together. The author's assumption was that a child's personality is set by the age of five. That leads to the conclusion that if you mess up as a parent during those first crucial years, it's over for your child. The prevailing emotion of several of our group was, "I've ruined my child." Fortunately, that month I had dipped into my stockpile of garage sale and used-book purchases to sample a few other books on the same subject. "Now wait," I said. "Let's see what someone else thinks about this." So I shared with them ideas from some other books. We found other ways to look at things. You can do that too, with or without a book club.

Another question I ask myself is, How does this advice or research compare with my experience? We live in a world of scientific advances and advantages, experts and specialists; to some extent we have been socialized to look to science for more and better answers. I had for many years felt that if my experience differed from what I read in a book, I should trust the expert. Now, however, I don't *substitute* expertise for my own experience; instead, I *measure* expertise *by* my experience.[3]

I am always careful, though, to separate description from prescription. Let me explain what I mean. Sometimes when I read over-the-counter advice books, the first few chapters will describe my own situation perfectly. I'll find myself saying, "That's me! That's just like me! Did they read my journal?" Because they describe my situation so accurately, I can get into dangerous territory if I accept the implications they draw as true or the prescriptions for changing the situation as good. For example, after describing my situation, the expert may tell me: "Now, take a foam baseball bat and beat the chair while imagining the person you are mad at sitting there." This expert advice, I guarantee you, is not in harmony with gospel teachings.

Having said that, I should reemphasize that I'm not against research, social science, and scholarly expertise. We know from scripture that we are to become acquainted with all good books (see D&C 90:15). And not all good books are written by LDS General Authorities. President Howard W. Hunter, citing Elder Orson F. Whitney, has taught us that many good people outside the Church, "possessing profundity of thought, great wisdom, and a desire to uplift their fellows, have been sent by the Almighty into many nations to give them . . . [a] portion of the truth."[4] Elder Neal A. Maxwell cautions that "the LDS scholar has his citizenship in the kingdom, but carries his passport into the professional world, not the other way around."[5] Your passport into the world of experts is your righteousness, your goodness, and the doctrines of the kingdom. Take that with you in your study of worldly philosophies and you can be inspired and have questions answered by some of these books. I have learned a great deal from insightful, moral family scholars such as Robert Bellah or Jean Elshtain or Parker Palmer and numerous others.[6]

As you ponder, study, sift, and pray to find insights, be prepared for spiritual answers that seem to contradict the experts. For example, one summer my daughter, who had been babysitting a lot, began missing money out of her drawer. I didn't suspect the older children—they had their own money—but two younger ones were candidates. I talked to both of them, gave them an opportunity to confess. They both determinedly professed their innocence. The money, however, kept disappearing. It was really creating a problem in our family, and I was at my wit's end. I knew that experts say never to accuse a child unless you are sure (good, sound advice!). So I prayerfully said, "Heavenly Father, I need to solve this problem, and you know who's taking the money." When I asked to know who it was, the name of one of my children came into my mind. I went to that child, in full confidence, and said, "I know you've been taking the money." He said, "How do you know that?" And I said, "I just know." He admitted, "You're right," opening the way for us to talk out the problem. My behavior went totally against expert advice, yet it worked because my insight came from a higher source.

The last discovery I've made, and the most important piece of advice I can pass on, is to enjoy your children. Researchers, after studying children before the age of five and then twenty years later, have found that "the most important influence in their lives—dwarfing all others—was how much their parents, especially their mothers, had loved them, had enjoyed them, and had shown affection for them."[7] Sometimes we feel so anxious about how they are turning out, or what kind of a job we're doing, that we can't stop the teeth gritting long enough to actually enjoy the dailiness (and sometimes mayhem) of family life. They will grow up. So in the meantime be patient with yourself, laugh and relax and enjoy your children. All the best "specialists" do.

NOTES

1. Joseph F. Smith, *Improvement Era* 7 (December 1904): 135.

2. Rex D. Pinegar, "Truth Is the Best Treatment," *AMCAP Journal* 9 (October 1983): 8.

3. I owe this insight to my friend and associate Dr. Terence D. Olson of the BYU Family Science Department.

4. Howard W. Hunter, "The Gospel—a Global Faith," *Ensign,* Nov. 1991, 19, citing Orson F. Whitney, in Conference Report, Apr. 1921, 32–33.

5. Neal A. Maxwell, "Some Thoughts on the Gospel and the Behavioral Sciences," *Ensign,* July 1976, 70.

6. I would recommend the following books by some of these authors:

    Robert N. Bellah, Richard Madsen, William M. Sullivan, Ann Swidler, and Steven M. Tipton, *Habits of the Heart: Individualism and Commitment in American Life* (New York: Harper & Row, 1985).

    Parker J. Palmer, *To Know As We Are Known: A Spirituality of Education* (San Francisco: Harper Collins, 1983).

    David Blankenhorn, Steven Bayme, and Jean Bethke Elshtain, eds., *Rebuilding the Nest: A New Commitment to the American Family* (Milwaukee, Wis.: Family Service America, 1990). This is a wonderful collection of essays, including one by Bruce Hafen, all having in common an acknowledgment of the moral dimension of family life.

7. Diane E. Papailla and Sally Wendkos Olds, *A Child's World: Infancy through Adolescence,* 6th ed. (New York: McGraw-Hill, 1993), 356.

MY LAST VISIT

ELISA PULIDO

The last time my grandparents came to visit
we found Grandma in Mother's closet
searching through skirts and dresses
for the front door.

And afterwards,
when we visited their ranch,
we found that Grandma's raisin cakes
refused to rise for want of baking powder
and that she put her best red glasses into the hutch
still greasy and crusted with last night's meal.
And she now insisted that her dislocated shoulder
was an arm completely severed
and reattached with black thread
by Dr. Lindsey in his one-room office.

I remember one afternoon there
when my sister and I and five or six cousins,
dodged cow pies and mosquitos
through Grandpa's back pasture
trying to catch his horse and a few sassy others,
that, given the chance,
would rub young riders' legs

Elisa Pulido graduated from Brigham Young University with a bachelor of arts degree in German and received a teaching credential from California State–San Bernardino. She also served a mission in the Switzerland Zurich mission. Elisa has three children and resides with her husband in Madrid, Spain, where she teaches seminary and serves on the stake public affairs committee.

into barbed-wire fencing.
These we trotted through sagebrush
until the white ranch house was but a small point
under an exclamation of low hills, white clouds.
I remember we laughed beneath that big sky,
when three cousins recited in unison,
the limb-restoring feat of the great Dr. Lindsey
after the manner of Grandma herself.
And, I remember the next morning, how
Grandma, her long white hair pulled back,
stood at her stoves—one coal, one electric—
cooking a breakfast of fried trout and eggs.
I sat trying to drink warm, raw milk
from a cloudy red glass, when she
scooped one egg
from a pot of boiling water
and laid it on my grandfather's empty plate.
His large, rough, rein-pulled hands
took a knife and cracked the shell—
clear whites, raw yolk spilled
onto his plate.

He slowly took a spoon and drank that egg
never once raising his pale hatless forehead
or bronzed jaw, shaven but never quite smooth.
His brown eyes bleached blue from seventy winters
on the glaring snow-covered Wyoming range,
refused to meet my round-eyed stare, would not see
my sister's half-smile.

But when he had swallowed
the last, he rose,
laid his large hand
on my grandmother's shoulder,
thanked her softly
and went to the barn.

THE CHALLENGE OF AGING ADULTS: THEIR CARE, YOUR CARE

BONNIE MUIRBROOK BLAIR

I need to begin with a disclaimer of sorts. In what I am about to share, please understand that the messenger still is struggling to understand the message. My other concern regards the private, personal nature of this experience—not only for myself but also for other family members, friends, and, especially, the person who received the care, whose story this is, too: my mother-in-law.

I met my mother-in-law for the first time while my husband, Frank, and I were dating, at her eightieth birthday party. I married Frank, who is several years my senior, when I was twenty-nine. I had been teaching high school and college for eight years. So when my mother-in-law came to live with us, we had been married only three years and had two sons, nineteen months and six weeks old. During the eight years she lived in our home, we added two daughters to our family, and my husband served as bishop, retired from his lifelong career, and started a new business. My father died, my mother served a mission and moved from her home of forty-five years into an apartment, and I served three years as stake Relief Society president. In short, it was a very demanding time in our lives.

Bonnie Muirbrook Blair received her master's degree in home economics education from Brigham Young University. A homemaker, she and her husband, Frank S. Blair, are the parents of four children. She is a school volunteer and a counselor in her ward Relief Society presidency.

The first time I remember considering the idea of Grandmother, as we all called her, coming to live with us was when Frank and I were drawing up our house plans. Frank asked how I would feel about designing the downstairs to be used as an apartment for his mother if she ever needed it. I don't recall having any objections at that time. I got along well with my mother-in-law, who had graciously and lovingly welcomed me into her family. I was very much in love with my husband and wanted to please him and be the perfect wife.

When the house plans were finished, we showed them to Grandmother. With the plans spread on her living room floor in front of her rocking chair, Frank explained the various rooms and details. She thanked us for thinking of her but said emotionally, "I would never live with my children. I have money set aside, and if the time comes that I can't live here in my own home, I will go to a rest home." She told us about a favorite aunt who had checked herself into a nursing home when she decided it was time and assured us she intended to do the same. I believed her. And, more important, I'm sure she believed herself.

We proceeded with our building plans, and soon we excitedly moved into our home. We landscaped the yard, shopped for furniture, and found we were expecting our first child. We usually spent Saturdays at Grandmother's, taking care of her house, yard, and the family land for which my husband was responsible. Caught up as I was with my new roles of wife and mother, I was probably not very sensitive to Grandmother's growing unrest. For the first time in her life, she was alone in her home most of the time. Businesses had sprung up across her once-rural street, yet the remaining farmland left her without close neighbors. I have vague memories of occasional calls at night when she was fearful that someone was in her yard. Caring friends told Frank that his mother was not doing well alone. Initially unwilling to consider selling her home of sixty years, Grandmother now agreed to have it put on the market.

85

I have a difficult time explaining my thinking processes at this point. I was aware that her home was for sale, and we must have talked about her coming to live with us. At the same time, no one seemed interested in buying her home, and I still remembered her earlier statements about not living with her children. I just didn't feel that change was imminent.

Perhaps my inability to focus on this event was partially due to my being pregnant again. When our second child was a few weeks old, my husband announced suddenly that Grandmother's home had a buyer who wanted to take possession in one month. In somewhat of a stupor (after all, I spent my nights up with a newborn and my days chasing a highly energetic toddler), I began to clean the downstairs, which had been vacant since we moved in. Frank's sister came from out of state to help Grandmother move and to clean the old house. She arranged furniture, bought needed items, got rid of some unneeded ones, and insisted on finding a weekly cleaning woman for her mother. For all of this I was very grateful.

At the time she came to live with us, Grandmother was eighty-three years old. She did her own cooking and laundry, drove her car, visited out-of-state family members about once a year, knit beautiful sweaters, read voraciously, keenly followed current events, and, most important, was a loving and concerned matriarch to her family. She maintained close contact with her children, grandchildren, nieces, and nephews through frequent phone calls and never let a birthday or anniversary pass without a card and check. She had reared four children and had contributed in time and energy to building the family businesses. A widow for seven years, she had given of herself freely in community and church service. Her husband, who had suffered from diabetes and its complications, had spent the last four years of his life in a nursing home; she was with him each day. She was a proud grandmother who loved her grandchildren and wanted to hear about and attend, whenever possible, their activities.

She walked with a cane, the result of a hip fracture a few years before Frank and I were married. She also had arthritis in her hip and back. Naturally, these slowed her down, and standing for very long was difficult. She was also beginning to have some problems with incontinence.

After the initial adjustment of having someone else living in our home, things went well. Our almost-two-year-old loved his visits downstairs. He and Grandmother read books, baked cookies, and took daily walks to the mailbox, weather permitting, to post her many cards and letters. I remember watching them out the window one morning, noticing that my son, using a stick for his cane, was walking with a limp like his grandmother's.

Grandmother enjoyed cooking and prepared herself a full meal every night, along with a good breakfast and lunch. She looked forward to grocery shopping and enjoyed watching cooking shows on television and trying new recipes. She baked delicious pies. She still canned some of her favorites—peaches, pickles, and her famous chili sauce. We joined her downstairs each week for Sunday dinner.

Change came gradually. First she became increasingly reluctant to drive. From our home, she had to enter a major highway to get anywhere, and our community was unfamiliar to her, about a twenty-minute drive by freeway from her former home. Not many months after moving in with us, she quit driving entirely.

Incontinence problems increased. Her arthritis bothered her more, and she began to spend more time in bed with her heating pad. Then, about eighteen months after her move, Grandmother fell and cracked her hip. Six months later, she fell again, hurting her wrist and hand. The next fall, just three months later, was the worst and resulted in a broken kneecap. Sitting was very painful; she had to wear an immobilizer and lie or stand most of the time. Our third child was due in about a month, and I felt overwhelmed and inadequate. A dear sister from our ward helped by coming to bathe Grandmother three times a week, a deeply appreciated service.

This was the spring of the floods in Utah. One morning the sister who bathed Grandmother noted as she walked in, "You know, Bonnie, you can see that mud slide on the mountain really well from your front porch." I followed her pointing finger to a mud slide, across a major highway and much higher than our home, but unnerving nevertheless. My baby was about a month old. I was still in my nightgown, and the boys weren't dressed either. I had about three clean diapers in the house. I've already described Grandmother's condition. I waited until my friend went downstairs and then burst into tears. As I tried to change and feed the baby, I decided that we would just have to drown, because there was no way I could get organized and get everybody out! Fortunately, evacuation wasn't necessary. I can laugh about it now, but I remember how I felt. I was totally unable at the time to deal with what was happening to me.

Gradually, with physical therapy and lots of determination, Grandmother learned to get around with a walker. Her cleaning woman was doing her laundry and preparing food to supplement the meals I was taking downstairs. Eventually, Grandmother was able to go grocery shopping with me again, something she really enjoyed because she could buy exactly what she wanted. When we returned home, I unloaded and put away her groceries and then my own. Her daughter and a granddaughter bought nearly all of her nongrocery items for her. This same granddaughter also brought her a dozen or more library books every three weeks.

This period of time was also my introduction to the world of bureaucratic medicine. Suddenly, part of our life was ruled by the unseen power that declared how many days of each kind of care Grandmother was eligible for and who could provide it. A thick folder of insurance and Medicare forms dominated my desk, along with the phone number of the office that was supposed to be able to explain them to me. It was a world that continually surprised and baffled me. Just when I thought I understood the rules, they changed. I resigned myself to trying to provide the information required and asking only the most pressing questions.

Things settled once more into a routine. As Grandmother regained some of her mobility, she was able to do more for herself. She enjoyed having the children sit on her bed for stories or games. Because she could no longer manage the stairs, she came upstairs only on rare special occasions, when my husband helped her walk outside and around to the front door. She attended church with us on Sunday and special family events but became more and more reluctant to go other places.

Grandmother had now been with us about three and one-half years. On the last day of Christmas vacation, we were all sleeping in. In that fog between sleep and waking, I could hear someone calling. My mother-reflexes kicked in automatically, and I jumped out of bed and ran to the children's rooms. All were sleeping peacefully; I was now wide awake and still heard someone calling. I finally realized the voice was coming from downstairs. "It's your mom! Come quick!" I called to Frank and hurried downstairs. I should probably qualify how quickly I hurried. I was six months pregnant. My timing—or Grandmother's—was amazing.

We found Grandmother on the floor in her living room, near her Christmas tree. She was in extreme pain and unable to move. The pain was centered in her upper leg. Frank called the doctor and then the ambulance. I got a blanket and pillow to make her more comfortable. I felt so helpless. Frank went to the hospital, and I stayed with the children. He called about an hour later to report that Grandmother had broken a hip that would require surgery and the placement of, in laymen's terms, nuts and bolts to hold the bones in place. The surgery was successful, and she was in the hospital about ten days.

We were told that she would require intensive physical

therapy to learn to walk again. She was unable to get in and out of bed on her own and needed full-time professional care. Frank chose a nursing home recommended for its excellent physical therapy program. Grandmother was adamantly against going. We promised that she could come home again as soon as she could walk. She went only because she had no other choice.

She was very unhappy in the nursing home. The blessing in disguise was that her unhappiness served as strong motivation. She was now eighty-seven years old and weak from her surgery and hospital stay, but she worked very hard at all the exercises and activities assigned by the therapist. I look back with admiration on her determination and strength.

I also look back with amazement at my own naiveté and lack of foresight. The signs clearly pointed toward problems in the future, but I failed to recognize or understand them. Grandmother wanted no part of the nursing home beyond what it took for her to learn to walk again. She paid an additional fee to have all her meals in her room instead of with other residents. She refused to attend any social or entertainment activities offered. She insisted on having a phone in her room, something that was frowned upon by the nursing home. Grandmother was always frugal, but again she paid the additional cost of a private room and a private phone line. One day she even phoned the front desk when the buzzer at her bedside didn't bring the desired response.

My husband, with rare exception, visited her daily. We took the children often in the evenings. Her visiting teachers usually visited weekly. Other family members stopped by when they could. Even so, those four months were difficult for her. She made many phone calls and asked almost daily when she could come home. Finally her doctor gave her a tentative discharge date, and the countdown began. Of course, two days before D-day, our youngest daughter was born. So, the new baby and I went home from the hospital the same day Grandmother went home from the nursing home.

Grandmother's daughter visited from out of the state for the first week. Grandmother was still having difficulty getting in and out of bed and dressing herself; she could not be alone. The days her daughter could stay elapsed, and Grandmother was still physically unable to take care of herself. The doctor and the therapist strongly urged her to return to the nursing home. With great reluctance she went back for about three more weeks.

Once Grandmother was home again, new challenges presented themselves. She still needed a lot of physical help. A physical therapist visited two or three times weekly. A home health care aide assisted with bathing. Getting in and out of a car was difficult and painful, so Grandmother's only trips out were to the doctor's office. Unsure on her feet, Grandmother was now frightened to attempt anything that didn't allow her to keep both hands on her walker. In addition to her physical limitations, the fall and ensuing events had taken an emotional toll as well. Always nervous about being alone, especially at night, she was now unwilling to be alone at all. She was depressed, lonely, and afraid, though I'm not sure I recognized those things at the time. I just knew that I couldn't provide for her all that she needed and wanted.

A simple call from Grandmother for me to come downstairs to help her frustrated and upset me. Should I go down alone, hoping to be there only a few minutes, and leave the children upstairs? Or should I haul all the kids with me, hoping they wouldn't get in the way if I need to help her into the bathroom? My children were now ages five, four, two, and two months. I felt torn and stretched beyond my capacities.

Grandmother's fears of being alone meant that even if we took all of the children with us, we still needed a sitter when we left our home. Sometimes family members and neighbors were available, but mostly we hired teen-aged girls for the company and to make sure she got to the bathroom or had her dinner. If my husband and I went somewhere alone, we were not sure a sitter could take care of four children and a grandmother. It was not unusual to come home and find the children still up, downstairs on Grandmother's bed playing games and watching TV with the sitter and Grandmother. If the children were in their beds, often the sitter was downstairs with Grandmother, out of earshot of the children's rooms. Grandmother strongly encouraged anything that would mean she wasn't alone.

Physical therapists, home health care workers, and hired people all helped Grandmother. The last year we also discovered Council on Aging volunteers. Some neighbors and ward members also helped. A local Girl Scout troop visited Grandmother and helped her organize and mount a box of loose photographs. One of the Young Women helped with Grandmother as her Laurel project. In our fast-growing area, our ward boundaries and leaders changed several times during the eight years. Because my husband was the bishop part of the time, and I was the stake Relief Society president the remainder, asking for help was somewhat awkward. I will always be grateful to the Relief Society presidents who called and organized ward sisters to visit Grandmother regularly. I'm not sure that someone who hasn't been in a similar situation can fully understand how much we appreciated any and all help.

Having expressed those sentiments, I must say in all honesty that having volunteers and paid help also added another dimension to my work. I became the master scheduler, responsible for keeping track of who was coming when, who would not be available, who canceled, who rescheduled—and arranging our family life around that. When I thought I had arranged for someone to be with Grandmother, then I would plan for errands, family outings, and appointments. When someone canceled or forgot, the dominoes began to fall, and the scheduler began rescheduling.

The most difficult aspect of this for me was being the employer, or personnel director. Frank or I would hire the personnel and explain their jobs, but Grandmother told them what she wanted done, and she paid them. As a result, often what we wanted was not what they actually did. I also discovered that I was not very good at maintaining employer-employee relationships. It was difficult for me to say "you must or must not" to helpers who were or soon became friends.

Having help also meant that people were in and out of our home a great deal. It was hard for me to adjust to the feeling that my home was not my own and that at any moment someone might be standing in my downstairs hall calling for me or coming up the stairs.

The demands of four small children, a busy husband, church callings, a fledgling family business, and Grandmother left me exhausted. I longed to wake up feeling rested. I was afraid that I wouldn't hear the baby at night because I was so tired. There just didn't seem to be enough of me to go around, but the only solution seemed to be to do more. I cried a lot and unloaded frustrations on a few close friends.

But my biggest challenge was my growing resentment and anger. Recognizing these feelings produced great guilt. I was sure I was not a good person because I resented the demands of caring for Grandmother. I was not serving with Christlike love. I knew I should repent and try to change. I prayed to have better feelings about my situation, but when I got up off my knees to a ringing phone or someone calling for me, the anger and resentment welled up inside me. I sat one Sunday in Relief Society, staring at the framed needlepoint sampler that declared, "Charity never faileth." Charity may never fail, I thought, but I'm failing. I felt ashamed, hopeless, and alone.

These were not easy times for Grandmother either. In addition to her leg and back pain, she was losing her hearing, becoming more incontinent, and having trouble breathing. She had been a strong, self-sufficient, private woman. Now, each day she was at the mercy of others for even her most basic needs. Much of the time when I felt Grandmother was being difficult, she was probably only trying to maintain some sense of dignity, self-respect, and control.

Grandmother's physical problems continued to mount. The breathing difficulties intensified until she was struggling for air, especially when lying down. She became extremely frightened about dying. She frequently phoned to beg me to come downstairs. "Sit here by me," she would say. "I don't want to die alone."

Still, she refused to see a doctor. Her distrust of medicine, doctors, and hospitals intensified. Finally, under coercion, she went for an exam and was diagnosed with congestive heart failure. Her heart could no longer pump efficiently; her lungs were filling with fluid. The doctor wanted to hospitalize her to reduce the fluid level with intravenous medication. "I am not going to the hospital," she said quietly but firmly. The doctor explained again. I reasoned with her. "I am not going to the hospital," she repeated. Finally, in desperation, I called my husband at work. Frank talked to the doctor, then to Grandmother, then to me. He came to take his mother to the hospital. After helping him get her into his car, I left. As I walked away, I could hear her say, "I'm not going to the hospital."

She stayed about a week. At home, she now needed oxygen and medication to keep the fluid down. She was weaker physically and emotionally. Her knitting needles lay idle, her library books unopened. Her hearty appetite and interest in food declined. Her fear of being alone became an obsession. Her only concern was who would be with her or how long she might have to be alone. She felt alone any time the chair next to her bed was empty.

One spring afternoon, I joined my children on the front lawn in a kickball game. We hadn't played for ten minutes when my neighbor hurried over. Grandmother had called him, believing we had left her home alone. She often told friends on the phone that she had been alone all day, when I had left her bedside just minutes before and was still in the adjoining room where I had told her I would be.

Visits from friends and family dwindled. Grandmother wasn't enjoyable company most of the time now. She mostly wanted us to sit next to her bed and reassure her that we weren't leaving. At this point we hired full-time help. Mary came four days a week, from eight to three. The fifth day a volunteer from the Council on Aging came. We were on our own for evenings and weekends.

She now needed help every time she went to the bathroom. Hallucinations were next. At night, alone in her room, she saw people coming out of the walls and ceilings. She called us on the telephone, begging us to come downstairs. Once there, we tried to reassure her that no one was in her room. We had just gotten back into bed upstairs when the phone rang again—and again and again throughout the night. After she called the neighbors at 2 A.M. one night, we started unplugging her phone at bedtime. Then she woke us yelling my husband's name, over and over, till we reached her bedside. I began to stay up and read, thinking getting up wouldn't be as hard if I weren't asleep when she called. Most often, I fell asleep in the chair.

Finally one Saturday, I was upstairs after giving Grandmother her lunch when the phone rang. I expected it to be her. Instead, the voice on the other end asked if we had an elderly relative somewhere who might need help. The caller had received several phone calls that day and many on previous days from an elderly woman trying to locate her son. Their phone number was similar to ours. In her confusion, Grandmother had misdialed not once but many times. The fear of being alone that had brought her to our home was now the reason she would leave. We had given all we could, and it was not enough. She needed twenty-four-hour, nonstop care.

We contacted a woman who cared for elderly people in her home, but after a visit there we realized that she would be unable to meet Grandmother's needs. We visited nursing homes and talked with friends who had family members in nursing homes. The morning came when my husband had to tell his mother that she was going to a nursing home. She was angry, hurt, and defiant. She refused to go, even as we packed her things. Once she was settled in her room there, however, she became almost complaisant, talking about what pictures she wanted where and what things she needed from home.

I came home filled with sadness and relief—and my constant companion, guilt. Now the guilt was even greater because of my relief and sense of final failure. The relative calmness in my home and the still rooms downstairs were constant reminders of what I had done and failed to do.

Grandmother seemed to do quite well the first couple of weeks in the nursing home. She complained about the food and what seemed like long waits for nurses. Frank visited her daily, and we took the children a couple of times a week. Relief Society sisters visited regularly. But then the confusion and hallucinations intensified. She had a difficult time remembering people and became more and more listless. She only picked at her food. She didn't want to get out of bed. Then one night the nursing home called, saying she hadn't eaten all day. I hurriedly prepared some of her favorite foods, and Frank took a plate to her. He returned just before midnight, having failed to get Grandmother to eat. She hadn't even opened her eyes while he was there. About noon the next day, the rest home notified us that Grandmother had died. It had been seven weeks since she had left our home.

The blessed numbness that often accompanies death arrived. I made phone calls, helped plan the funeral, ordered flowers. Family members arrived; neighbors called. I went through all the motions, doing for the most part all I was supposed to do. I didn't allow myself to think or feel too deeply. My feelings were jumbled, and trying to sort them out hurt too much. When everybody had gone home, I returned to a daily routine and worked hard not to think about all that had happened. In effect, I closed the door on that part of my life. Reopening it has been difficult and sometimes painful but has allowed the healing process to begin.

What have I learned? Caring for a family member is a family affair. All immediate family members should contribute in some way and be involved in decision making, even those living away from where the care will be given. I recommend consulting books that outline the process a family should go through when making major caregiving decisions.[1] We also should have planned for and talked about the circumstances under which we would no longer be able to care for Grandmother.

Studies show that "the degree of satisfaction experienced by caregivers did not relate to the number of hours they put in or the number of people they cared for, but rather to *the caregiver's ability to care for themselves.*"[2] Caregivers who care for themselves as well as they care for another person are likely to be the most successful. For many of us, distinguishing between self-care and selfishness is difficult. At some point during my caregiving experience, I crossed the line into self-neglect, and both Grandmother and I suffered. I wish I had been more willing to accept and able to express my need for self-care earlier. What I saw as failure at the time was, in many cases, simply burnout. I was totally spent, both emotionally and spiritually. It has been an arduous, private journey back to spiritual and emotional well-being.

Admitting my resentment, anger, and guilt publicly is still not easy. Part of the learning process for me has been to understand that I do have weaknesses; they do not go away simply because I want them to. I now know that developing

97

charity, empathy, self-respect, and personal strength will be a lifelong work for me—as it is for everyone. I have also learned that charity, the pure love of Christ, is a gift that comes after "pray[ing] unto the Father with all the energy of heart" (Moroni 7:48). I thought I had to develop it all by myself.

In the Church we often hear that caring for the elderly develops Christlike love. I'm not sure that happened to me during the caregiving experience. As a caregiver my feelings were often very negative. I have tried to be honest about how difficult the experience was, about how troubled I have been that I was not able to serve all of the time with Christlike love.

In Matthew 5:48 we are told, "Be ye therefore perfect, even as your Father which is in heaven is perfect." A footnote explains that the word *perfect* was translated from a Greek word meaning complete, finished, fully developed. My caregiving experience is part of my mortal effort to become like our Heavenly Father. But I was not complete, finished, or fully developed when I did it. I was learning, and like most students, I lacked understanding of some of the concepts and struggled with some of the assignments. Some days I didn't even want to go to school. But I now understand that I didn't fail the final exam. I have learned much about empathy, compassion, and acceptance of my own and other's weaknesses and struggles. I believe I am better prepared for future learning experiences. And I am comforted that my care allowed my mother-in-law to live a more fulfilling life.

Friends have asked, "Would you do it again?" I have thought long and hard about that question. I hope I wouldn't ever have to, at least under the same circumstances. But I took on the care of my mother-in-law because I love my husband, and it was very important to him that we care for his mother. That love continues, stronger than before. Yes, I would do it again.

If you know someone who is a caregiver, take time to find out how they are doing. Look for ways, even small ones, to help. And please, reserve judgment. What they are doing is probably more difficult than it appears. And if you are the caregiver, please take care of yourself, seek help from others, accept that you will be angry and resentful at times, and remember that, imperfect as you feel it may be, your service is invaluable.

NOTES

1. Two such books are Rosalynn Carter and Susan K. Golant, *Helping Yourself Help Others: A Book for Caregivers* (New York: Random House, 1994), and Jo Horne, *Caregiving: Helping an Aging Loved One* (Glenview, Ill.: Scott, Foresman, and Co., 1985).

2. Carter and Golant, 47.

A QUILT OF CARE: ASSISTING OLDER PEOPLE IN NEED

COSETTE MILLS

Older people come in diverse shapes, textures, and colors. For some, time has worn the fabric of their lives, necessitating outside reinforcement. Caring for these frail individuals can be as challenging as stitching together a Triple Irish Chain or Double Wedding Ring.

We can be better prepared to help the aged if we first understand demographic trends for older people in the United States.[1] What do statistics tell us? More people are living longer. In 1900, life expectancy was about forty-seven years; today people can generally expect to reach age seventy-six—an increase of twenty-nine years. The longer people live, the more likely they are to need assistance. We should be particularly aware of older women—who are more likely to live alone because they live longer than men. By age eighty-five and above, there are 256 women to every 100 men. We should also note that both older women and minority individuals are at greater risk, because they are more likely to have lower incomes.

Consider other characteristics of United States society today that affect frail, older citizens. Families are changing. They are

Cosette W. Mills received her bachelor of science degree in family relations, gerontology emphasis, from Weber State College. She and her husband, Brent B. Mills, are the parents of four children. She has worked for several organizations serving older persons and serves as education counselor in her ward Relief Society.

more mobile than ever, have fewer children, and more women are working. Caregivers of the past lived at home. Frequently now, they are either not available or they must sandwich the care they give between jobs and their own families.

Communities are changing as well. Neighbors do not know each other as they once did. Socializing or visiting is less common as a form of leisure. Homes are often empty during the day. Life is fast-paced, full of stress. All around us we see more focus on self and less focus on serving others.

Individual wellness and changes in health care must also be considered. Most men and women over sixty-five have one or more chronic conditions, although most adapt to these conditions without help. Twenty-three percent need help with personal care, such as bathing, dressing, eating, moving from bed or chair, walking, or toileting. Twenty-eight percent need help with meal preparation, shopping, managing money, and housework. Of those over the age of eighty-five, 58 percent need assistance with some of these activities. And for those that need health care, hospital stays are shorter and patients are often sent home needing extensive and highly technical in-home care. Health care costs have also risen dramatically, hitting the older population especially hard. In 1987, persons sixty-five and older represented 12 percent of the U.S. population but accounted for 36 percent of personal health care expenditures.

Considering all these factors, how do we better address the needs of the elderly in our society, in our church, in our families? I suggest that we liken care for a frail, older person to a patchwork quilt. For a quilt to be warm and beautiful, the fabric blocks need to be carefully prepared, pieced together, and lovingly stitched. Similarly, when an older person needs care, specific needs must be conscientiously considered, arranged, and coordinated in a compassionate and loving way. Spiritual, social, physical, emotional, and mental needs should be carefully assessed. For some, the pattern is simple, requiring just a few blocks. Others have more intricate needs, requiring many precisely placed pieces.

Caring comes in varying proportions from three important sources: the older individuals themselves; an informal support network of family, church, neighbors, and friends; and formal programs available in the community. All too often, care for older persons seems to have been thrown together, leaving gaps and holes. And sometimes, the love to tie it all together is missing.

The first and most essential block for our quilt of care is the older person. The Church encourages principles of self-reliance, and we must allow individuals to do all they safely can for themselves or we will destroy their self-esteem. But how do we know how much help to give? Take cues from the individual and in some cases from the family. In most instances, if older people know and trust you, they will tell you what they need help with when your questions to them are specific. For example, instead of asking: "Do you need help with anything?" say, "Is it difficult for you to carry your laundry up and down the stairs?"

Frail, older persons may work slowly, and their work may not be up to their previous standards. That is not important as long as they are in no danger and are able to work. We should make every effort to encourage their independence, allowing them to live in their own homes and do as many of their own tasks as possible for as long as possible.

The second essential block is an informal support network. Most of the help older people receive (60 to 80 percent) comes from an informal support source such as the family or church. In my experience, successful caregiving families do many things in common. Many family members share in the caregiv-ing duties, instead of the load falling on one person. The families meet and plan in councils that include the older persons. The families consider the resources and strengths of each member and figure out ways for those living away from home to contribute. Last, when they need outside help, they get it.

Sometimes, however, families run into problems. Often as the older person's functioning becomes more limited, families have difficulty acknowledging that they can't do everything. If they don't get help, they often burn out or become ill, stressing the family even more. At other times, care cannot be provided safely in the home, and an institution becomes appropriate.

In families that have never gotten along well, involving family members in care may create increased pain and frustration. Abuse or neglect is also a potential problem in such a situation. In addition, some older people don't want their families to know their problems and concerns, and some families don't want to hear about them.

Neighbors, friends, and wards can do a lot to help care for the elderly. I have been surprised on numerous occasions to find that the ward wasn't providing help or the older person didn't perceive the ward as wanting to provide help. I believe the Church can support older persons in many ways, supplementing what the individuals themselves and their families can do. Ward councils may carefully consider the spiritual, social, physical, mental, and emotional needs of each older person within its boundaries, realizing the wealth of Christlike service opportunities available and recognizing the great resource older persons can be to a ward. Here are a few suggestions about how we as Church members might help in each area of need.

SPIRITUAL NEEDS

Spiritual growth can continue at all ages. Many find in their later years deeper levels of refinement and commitment to spiritual convictions. Spiritual activity without the support of others, however, can be lonely and discouraging. What can Church members do to enhance the spiritual needs of the elderly? We can ensure that older members have access to the

103

Church News and Church magazines. A member could read aloud to those who are visually impaired. Visiting and home teachers could more actively look for ways to add spirituality to the older person's life, such as visiting with better prepared messages, praying with the individuals at the end of a visit, or offering priesthood blessings. Family home evening groups could be established or families in the ward could invite older persons to join with them. Ward auxiliary groups could take lessons into the homes of older ward members.

When I was a Beehive adviser, once a month our class held our lesson, activity, and refreshments at the home of two older sisters in our ward. Each session was inspiring as these sisters shared their wisdom, testimonies, humor, and gratitude. The young women benefited as much as the older sisters did!

Priesthood members could administer the sacrament at the home of older ward members unable to attend sacrament meeting. In addition, bishops could try to find meaningful ward assignments that use older persons' talents and enhance their spiritual growth.

SOCIAL NEEDS

Loneliness is one of the greatest problems frail, older people face. Imagine what it's like to be home nearly twenty-four hours a day. One call or visit per day may still leave a person alone for more than twenty-three hours. No wonder feelings of loneliness or discouragement are so prevalent. What can members of the Church do to help? Visiting and home teachers can plan longer or more frequent visits and avoid appearing rushed. Consistent visits early in the month show visiting isn't a burden. Unassigned visits are important also. Older ward members are particularly good visitors. If visiting isn't possible, daily calls can be made by and to older members. Because they don't want to worry their family members, some elderly people will talk more freely to people outside their families.

In conversations with the elderly, let them lead out, expressing needs or sharing wisdom. Allow them—encourage them—to reminisce or grieve. Offer to visit weekly to help record their life history. Take them on outings whenever possible. Pick them up and accompany them to church and other activities or take them for a ride. Invite them to Sunday dinner. Or, if you take a meal, offer to eat with them. Better still, arrange to take in the meal ingredients and then prepare the food and eat together. Meal times without others can be particularly lonely.

PHYSICAL NEEDS

Physical needs include individual care as well as care for the home, finances, and essential transportation. These kinds of needs often require consistent, continuing support and help. For older people needing a little assistance to bathe and dress themselves, ward members could provide "stand-by" assistance to prevent falling or to assist with fastening clothing. Relief Society sisters could modify clothes for easier dressing using velcro rather than buttons or front zippers rather than back. For those who may need more extensive assistance from a trained aide, professional home health services could be arranged.

Another type of assistance frequently needed is care of the home and yard. It can be discouraging for older persons to look through dirty windows or see a carpet in need of vacuuming and not be able to do the work themselves. Regular assistance with heavier household tasks such as changing linens on beds, vacuuming, mopping, and laundry can be offered, remembering not to take away tasks the older persons can manage on their own. Also, an elderly person may need help with weekly lawn care, flowers, mail, home repairs, and weatherization. Ice and snow removal are especially important to prevent isolation, falls, and serious injury. In addition, some older persons on fixed incomes often have financial worries. Frequently they will pay bills before buying food or medications. They may require financial or food assistance to meet the most basic needs. They also may lack transportation to buy groceries, visit the doctor, shop, or attend other events. Invite them along when you are going out, or ask specifically about their transportation needs.

EMOTIONAL AND MENTAL NEEDS

Depression and discouragement are common among the less mobile elderly. A listening ear, a visit, or a hug can do a lot to brighten a day. Be alert for signs of serious depression or emotional problems and also watch for confusion or disorientation. Professional treatment should be sought for such conditions. Observing if these conditions come on suddenly or gradually can help in getting appropriate treatment.

Emotional needs of caregivers also need to be considered. Caregivers are at great risk for burnout when providing constant care. They need a respite at least weekly to rest, run errands, or do something just for themselves. With consistent relief, caregivers can usually function much longer and much more effectively, without destroying their own health.

Opportunities for learning or teaching can also provide a great boost. Older sisters may have wonderful skills and insight to share with younger sisters during homemaking meetings. Again, specific questions may unlock treasures. Not "What skills do you have?" but "Do you have a favorite recipe for holiday fruit cake? Will you teach us how to make it?"

The third block of our quilt of care is community assistance. Resources from formal government or community programs are particularly important when skilled help is needed for safe care or when needs are longer term. Some available resources may include home health care, hospice (in-home support for the terminally ill), meals at a senior center or home delivered, adult day care, and institutionalization when twenty-four-hour care is needed. Availability of these services will vary from community to community and from state to state. It is also important to realize that many of these programs face major cuts in funding. Additionally, as the population of older persons increases, the ability of formal services to respond to the demand will likely decrease. In the future, older persons may need to depend on informal supports of family and church even more than today.

In James 1:27 we read: "Pure religion and undefiled before God and the Father is this, To visit the fatherless and the widows in their affliction." Giving this help, even when we want to, is not easy. Our lives may be busy and the extent of care required may seem overwhelming. But if we will use all the quilt pieces—including the older persons themselves, family, church, and other informal supports, and, when necessary, formal government and community programs—and then tie our quilt of care with love, together we will bless the lives of older persons, doing as our Savior would do.

NOTE

1. Demographics and statistical information were taken from *A Profile of Older Americans, 1994,* published by AARP and the Administration on Aging, based on information from the 1993 census.

ENJOY TO THE END

GWEN SQUIRES

As we move into the middle years of our lives, we may find that our circumstances are not what we had anticipated. Some women may be alone and looking for ways to fill their empty days. Others may have days that are too full and feel oppressed by many demands. Whatever our circumstances, we have the option to choose our attitude toward them. We can choose to let them overwhelm and defeat us, or we can choose to find the beauty, humor, and good in each day. This was recently reaffirmed to me when my eldest daughter, a stake Primary president, shared with me the theme they had selected for stake leadership meeting—"enjoy to the end." When I find myself in an endurance frame of mind, I try to switch to an "enjoy the moment" attitude. I believe that Heavenly Father meant for us to find joy in this life.

In my fifties I returned to school after a thirty-year absence to complete a master's degree in social work. At age fifty-five, my husband, an air traffic controller, was approaching retirement. With eight of our ten children still at home, and five adult retarded women (we refer to them as our foster girls) also living with us, I was not looking for ways to fill my days. This seemed, however, to be the right time to return to school.

Three of our ten children were born after I was forty. I was

Gwen Forsyth Squires is a licensed clinical social worker at the American Fork Hospital. She and her husband, Ray Squires, are the parents of ten children. She serves as stake Young Women president.

having such a good time with the children that I missed my cue to stop. In fact, Sara came into the world already an aunt a month before my forty-seventh birthday. One day when she was still very tiny, I was tending my two grandchildren when the phone rang. My grandson Andy ran to answer it and to my dismay I heard him say, "Grandma can't come to the phone right now. She's nursing the baby." I am thankful I never learned who the caller was.

I had done a year's work toward a master's degree in social work and had planned to go back to school. The time had come. I'll never forget the day I went to the registrar's office at the University of Utah to get a copy of my transcript of credits. The room was crowded, and my husband, of course, was standing next to me. The woman behind the counter said to me in a very loud voice, "What year did you say you were here?" I repeated the year I had last been in school. She sighed, "We'll have to go to the archives to get those records." My husband laughed. I didn't. I suddenly felt quite ancient and wondered if I was up to this new venture.

I decided to pursue my graduate studies at Brigham Young University. I was quite frustrated when they disregarded my previous year of study and required that I start the program over. My irritation dissipated, however, when I discovered that after thirty years I had no idea what the instructors were talking about. I crammed unfamiliar terms into the margins of my notes, hoping nobody would notice, and then hurried home to look them up. I felt overwhelmed and discouraged.

I hit my low point the day my first major paper was due. My professor, dean of the college, had emphasized on the first day of class: "Don't any of you think that your difficult circumstances will earn you any special consideration. We expect everyone to turn all work in on time." I immediately assumed he was speaking just to me. I remember thinking, He thinks I can't do this. And I seriously wondered if I could. I worked hard on researching my topic and felt reasonably well prepared to write the paper. That week was homecoming at American Fork High School, and my daughter Stacey, a sophomore, had been chosen as the second attendant to the homecoming queen. Wednesday morning, just as I was dashing out the door to class, she informed me, "Mom, I'm supposed to wear a white formal in the parade today." Two older sisters had previously been attendants, but their formals had been red—we had no white formals. I went to school frustrated and shared the problem with some classmates. "Gwen," they said, "we'll just call a few rental places and find one." Everyone got on a phone, and we located a white, size-four formal. After class I picked up the dress, rushed home, and found Stacey patiently waiting in her slip in the family room, never doubting I would come through for her. We zipped her into the dress, and she made it to the parade.

The next hurdle was the dance on Friday. My paper was due Friday. I suggested hopefully to Stacey, "Maybe you could wear Sabrina's dress, dear?" She didn't look convinced. No, I thought, she needs her own dress. I can handle this and my paper. So we went shopping on Thursday night. We shopped and shopped. I was very patient, but Stacey couldn't find anything she liked and finally said, "Maybe I could wear Sabrina's dress." At 9:30 we went home empty-handed. I thought, I can still handle this. I have my information, and I will stay up all night to type it. Then my three-year-old got sick. I sat with that three-year-old trying to type my paper. The first pages were really quite strong, but by four o'clock in the morning, as the baby would throw up and I would clean her up once again, my paper got weaker and weaker. Sometimes my fingers slipped to the wrong typewriter keys, and the words became a bit garbled.

I was sure I had no option but to turn the paper in. Hadn't my professor said there would be no exceptions? I got to class on time with the paper. A few students turned in papers; I was one of them. When I got the paper back, my professor's comments on the first few pages were complimentary, then came the red marks, and finally no marks at all. There was a note at the end: "You must have been very tired, my dear." I went home and wept. I wept like a first grader. From there I had nowhere to go but up.

Things did get better. The cobwebs cleared in my mind, and I moved forward. I learned how to manage my time. I took notes with me everywhere I went. In January we had to memorize the entire DSM-III, the *Diagnostic and Statistical Manual of Mental Disorders.* At Stacey's New Beginnings program at church I pretended to pay attention while studying my note cards. Someone said my name. I thought they were calling on me to say the closing prayer, so I stood up and said it. They weren't.

I learned to do all my studying in the early mornings. If I tried to stay up at night, the children stayed up to visit with me; nobody wanted to talk to me at 3:00 A.M. Our foster girls don't have a good sense of time, though. I was always very careful to be quiet so they wouldn't hear me and think it was time to get up. One morning I was up particularly early to study for a very important test. Unfortunately, the girls had been roused too, so I fixed their breakfast and then started studying. But eating breakfast didn't keep them occupied. "What are we going to do for Valentine's Day, Gwen?" I patiently told them. They then cycled through every birthday and holiday. I was getting less patient and more frustrated. Finally I said, "Girls, I have an important test to study for. Please don't bother me any more. We'll talk about this later." In a minute one of the girls came in and asked, "Gwen, what are we going to do for Christmas?" It was the last straw. I looked at her and said, "If one more person says one more word to me, I'm canceling Christmas." They didn't, and I didn't.

Despite all the distractions, graduate school worked out all right. In fact, I now look back on it as a period with its own particular joys and satisfactions. I finished my classes quite

111

respectably. I don't say that with pride; I say that to illustrate that women in midlife do have skills. We can compete.

I thought, Now I've got it made. Then I started a new job. I am a social worker at the American Fork Hospital. I assist families dealing with grief over the death of loved ones; I help abused women find courage to change their situations; I encourage suicidal patients to find new hope and resources to overcome their depression. It is a wonderful job. Each day brings its own challenges and rewards. In the beginning, however, I found once again that I didn't know what I was doing. Again I resorted to writing down unknown terms, this time medical terms, on the paper I kept secretly tucked away in my pocket. At home I looked up meanings. The medical staff hadn't had a full-time medical social worker before and didn't know what I was to do. Worst of all, I didn't know either. That, too, worked out. I couldn't ask for a better job. I have respect for and give respect to the excellent staff members I work with, and I find joy in my daily associations. Again I thought, now I've got it made.

Not for long. The new stake president of our recently divided stake asked me to be the stake Young Women's president. Was he aware, I mumbled, that I had a large family, worked full-time, and cared for five handicapped women? He smiled at me in his confident, capable manner and said, "Yes, we know that, Sister Squires," and went on to outline my responsibilities. I felt dismayed. That word kept running through my mind, Dismayed. I am so dismayed.

My first task was to select counselors, but I couldn't even remember who was in my stake. We had new boundaries. Finally I asked my husband to go to the temple with me. I was sure neon lights were going to go on, all the answers would flash before me, and I'd know just who to call to be my counselors. It didn't happen. Instead, as we waited in the chapel for our session to begin, a sister sat down at the piano. She played "How Firm a Foundation," and the words just jumped at me. "Fear not, I am with thee; oh, be not dismayed, / For I am thy

God and will still give thee aid."[1] I thought, How could I have forgotten that? This isn't my church. This isn't my program. This is Heavenly Father's program. He'll take care of me. . . . And he has. I have found another dimension of joy as I work with my counselors in this exciting, sometimes demanding, calling.

Being a grandmother also brings its own measure of joy. Because we don't have to be on the front lines of parenting these children, we are in a unique position to offer unconditional love and complete acceptance. I was acquainted with a gracious woman whose grandchildren's lives were tumultuous. She could do little to change their situations, but she could give them unconditional love, and she did. One day her sixteen-year-old granddaughter came to her house as a first step in running away from home. They talked into the wee hours of the morning and worked out the problem. Then this wise grandmother packed a suitcase, set it on the top shelf of her closet, and said, "Lisa, if you ever think you need to leave home again, come and get me and I will go with you."

Last week when I drove home, a three-year-old grandchild ran out to meet me with his hand tightly clenched. He thrust his closed fist at me and said, "Surprise! Guess!" I ventured, "A rock? A bug?" Chase laughed, opened his grubby little fist, and said, "It's for you." It was a crumpled-up dandelion. Joy comes in simple things.

I've had some wonderful experiences in my later life, returning to school, entering the professional work force, tackling an intimidating church calling, and loving and learning from my grandchildren. Some of these experiences were not what I had anticipated at this stage in life. Each of them has, however, brought me joy.

NOTE

1. *Hymns of the Church of Jesus Christ of Latter-day Saints* (Salt Lake City: The Church of Jesus Christ of Latter-day Saints, 1985), no. 85.

WHEN I WAS FIFTY-ONE

IONE J. SIMPSON

When I was fifty, my husband Del and I lived in Idaho Falls. We had five children: one married, one on a mission, two at Brigham Young University, and one a senior in high school. We owned our own business and worked hard making it successful. We were a happy family. Del and I were nearing the time in our lives when the heavy responsibility of raising a family was easing. When we talked about what the future held for us, Del often said he wished he could serve the Lord full time. We looked forward to going on a mission together.

When I was fifty-one, Del and I, four other stake presidents and their wives, and a Church visitor from Salt Lake, went on an outing to Island Park in Idaho. We were boating down the Snake River when our canoe overturned in the swift current, and Del was drowned. In a matter of minutes, I was a widow. It is impossible to express my pain. Only one who has had the experience can know the anguish and sorrow of that time.

Wise friends counseled me to make no important decisions for at least a year, and I followed their counsel. It was a time of grieving, of adjustment, and of planning. The years ahead had seemed so safe and sure. This would be like starting over again. I knew I needed to do something where I could be with

---

Ione J. Simpson received her master's degree in social work after the death of her husband and worked for LDS Social Services for ten years. She is the mother of six, grandmother of thirty-two, and the great-grandmother of six. She has served on the Relief Society General Board and teaches Gospel Doctrine in her ward.

and help people. Counseling appealed to me, but that would mean going back to school. Before I married, I had completed two years of college and then had gone on a mission. The very thought of going back to school terrified me. Could I study? Could I take tests? Could I compete with younger students? It had been almost thirty years since I had been in the classroom.

When I was fifty-two, I went back to school. First, I took just one class at Ricks College. Then I enrolled at Idaho State University and commuted three days a week with other "older" women students, still wondering if I could make it. I studied constantly. I'll never forget my first test. I had stayed up most of the night studying. When I got to class the sociology teacher announced that it would be a computer test, and I panicked. I had studied for a sociology test. What was a computer test? I was too embarrassed to ask questions because it was obvious the other students knew what she was talking about. When I finally got the test and read the directions, I realized the teacher was talking about a *computer-graded* test. I recovered my bearings, took the test, and passed.

At the end of a successful semester, I decided to finish my degree at Brigham Young University. I closed my home and found an apartment in Provo. Every credit I had earned thirty years before was still good, and I was a junior. One of the greatest blessings of school was that I didn't have time to feel sorry for myself. My days and nights were filled with studying. Learning was immensely satisfying.

By now we had had two more weddings in our family, and all of us were at a university. At one time, three of my children and I were enrolled at BYU at the same time. The two married daughters seemed pleased to have me there, but the youngest, who was unmarried, was not at all sure she liked going to the university with Mother.

By Christmas of the second year at BYU, I needed only three credits to graduate. I arranged to take the three hours by correspondence and joined thirty-four young people and one

115

other woman my age on a semester abroad in Israel for six exciting months. Upon my return to school, my three correspondence credits were accepted, and I marched with the other graduates to get my degree. Goal number one had been accomplished.

In the meantime, our home in Idaho Falls had stood empty for two years except for summers and holidays, when we gathered to be a family again. It looked as though I would not return to live in Idaho Falls, so I sold my home to my oldest son and bought a condominium in Salt Lake City.

When I was fifty-five, I began graduate school at the University of Utah. I had all kinds of experiences there: difficult ones, humorous ones, and challenging ones. But in two years, the day finally came that I could put on my cap and gown and graduate with a master's degree in social work. My first job after graduation was with LDS Social Services. I worked first with unwed mothers and then with adoptive parents. Helping deserving couples prepare for their families and then placing newborn infants in their arms was pure joy. I felt I had found my niche and spent nine fulfilling years there.

When I was sixty-six, I was invited to go to Washington, D.C., to act as director of policy for the National Committee for Adoption. It sounded like an exciting adventure, and even though I knew no one in Washington, I packed my clothes in my car and drove east with my son. We found an apartment for me close to my work, and he flew home.

At times my stay in Washington turned out to be more exciting than I had bargained for. That huge, beautiful city is without question the easiest place in the United States to get lost in. For someone directionally disabled, as I am, it was a challenge. On weekends, however, my sister who lived in Connecticut often came to Washington; together we visited the Smithsonian Institution, strolled down the Washington Mall (not a shopping center), boarded a bus and toured D.C., and traveled to fascinating historical spots in Washington, Virginia, and

Maryland. My supervisor commented that I saw more of this part of the country in one year than he had seen in his nineteen years there.

When I was sixty-seven, while still in Washington, D.C., I was called to be a member of the Relief Society General Board. Upon my return to Salt Lake from Washington, I worked for a year part-time for LDS Social Services while also serving on the board. As I served, primarily with welfare services, I learned of the great strength and devotion of my sisters throughout the Church.

Not until I was seventy-two did I face retirement. How do you slow down after so many years of constant activity? For a short time it was hard, but I have found many exciting things to do. When you don't *have* to do anything, the opportunities are limitless. I've spent several years on family genealogy, I have written my husband's life story, and I have traveled to fascinating countries. Most rewarding has been my greater involvement with my children and grandchildren. My five children live in four different states—none of them Utah. My thirty-two grandchildren range from eight years old to married with small children.

Sometimes we feel that as grandmothers we are past the time when we can influence children and grandchildren. I'm finding that's not so. If being together in eternity is our goal, we need to practice now. We need to love each other and enjoy being together. I figure I have more time to make this happen than anyone else.

Every two years we have family reunions with a different family in charge each time. One year we rented a large bus with video screens, a table for games, and a microwave in the back. Thirty of us traveled from Utah to the Palmyra pageant in New York, visiting Church and historical sites. We would have Captain Crunch and orange juice for breakfast in a park; sandwiches and soda pop for lunch in a parking lot; and often we stopped at Denny's or McDonalds for dinner.

Parents occupied the front seats of the bus and laughed and reminisced about their growing up years; teenagers were in the middle with their delightful and sometimes noisy entertainment; youngsters played games in the back. A time of rejoicing: I'm sure the only reunion that will top this one will be when we all meet again in the eternities.

Seven of the grandchildren are presently at Ricks College. Five married grandchildren attend BYU or the University of Utah. We hold family home evenings in my home once a month. Sometimes, such as at general conference, they all end up at my home. I make it as inviting as possible by keeping food on hand that they like but can't always afford, games they like to play, a bed or floor to sleep on, and a comfortable place to bring their friends. At every opportunity I let them know that I love them and remind them that our family goal is to share eternity together.

Now at age seventy-eight, let me tell you what I feel has made my life rich after fifty.

First, I am firmly convinced that we came to this earth to succeed. Heavenly Father knows us better than we know ourselves. He knows our strengths and our weaknesses. He will help us build on our strengths and overcome our weaknesses, if we ask him. Every one of us will have challenges. We can let those challenges control us, or we can take charge. My greatest strength has come from my faith that this is true. I find direction and confirmation in the scriptures.

Second, don't be content to do the easy thing. Look for opportunities to stretch farther than you think you can. Going back to school was a frightening experience at first, but succeeding brought tremendous satisfaction. Also, I found that my practical experience as a wife, mother, and church worker gave me an edge over younger, less experienced students.

Third, several years before my husband died, he and I sat down together and talked about our finances. I knew what insurance policies we had and what they could do for me. I knew about Social Security, savings, and indebtedness; I had even gone to the safety deposit box in the bank and knew what it contained. Very few couples do that. Often a widow is left with no idea about her financial circumstances. Wise planning can make all the difference in whether or not you will have a good life after fifty.

Fourth, develop a good attitude. It is so easy to feel sorry for yourself. Don't. All you have to do to become unpleasant company is to talk about your ailments or about how you couldn't sleep last night. I learned through experience that no matter what your problem, someone else will top your story. Forget about yourself. One good way to do that is to do something for someone else. Volunteer regularly for a worthwhile cause, make a telephone call, visit someone who needs you.

Last and most important, many times you will feel alone, but you never are. Your Heavenly Father will always be there. He knows your potential better than you do and will help you through your trials and your joys.

Perhaps it sounds as though my life has been easy. It has not. Like everyone else, I have been depressed. I have felt, Why me? and have had times when I was so lonely I didn't want to get out of bed, times when I could have stayed home and cried—and sometimes I did. It got me nowhere.

One very important thing I know—I am responsible for my own happiness. Every once in a while I have to learn that over again, but I work at it. Life is good! These later years are the very best years of life when we have the time to really concentrate on what is most important—loving and caring about those around us.

THAT FAST

ELAINE W. CHRISTENSEN

Sun warms the carpet at my feet.
Elongated window panes
pattern themselves across the floor.
The clock ticks.
In a back bedroom someone turns on a radio
and the cat comes, curious,
to see me sitting in the sun.

I am counting Septembers:

the one when she was born
her head, square,
her nose pushed flat,
her hands clasped, praying

the one when she entered kindergarten
her hair in braided loops
her face at the bus window
her face in her eyes

the one when she carried Grandma's
violin to her first day
of junior high orchestra
with the dreaded Miss Mahanah

Elaine Christensen, recipient of the Utah Poet of the Year award in 1990 for her book *At the Edges,* received her bachelor's degree from Utah State University in German and English. She and her husband, Roger P. Christensen, have five children. Elaine teaches Gospel Doctrine in her ward and is an institute instructor at Salt Lake Community College.

the one when she turned sixteen
and drove down the hill
in her new, used car,
down-shifting, radio blaring

Four Septembers. Weren't there more?

The cat comes whining for breakfast.
In a back bedroom, drawers open, close.
She is packing.
The sun is hot now at my feet.
The window patterns on the carpet
have straightened and squared themselves.
That fast. The clock has been ticking
that fast all this time.

REJOICING IN ONE ANOTHER'S ACHIEVEMENTS

NEILL MARRIOTT

I want to talk about feeling resentment or envy when a friend loses twenty pounds and you don't. I want to share my feelings with those not able to have a child who feel guilty about your bitterness when your sister announces her fourth pregnancy. I want to reach your hearts if you are wondering why you have to struggle with a less-active spouse or rebellious child while your neighbor doesn't.

What do we do with these feelings? I sometimes have had moments of jealousy, self-doubt, and inferiority when I have seen the achievements of others. I have looked away, hardening my heart, when a friend's daughter walked by wearing a beautifully sewn Easter dress. What an achievement for a busy mother of six! But I can't sew, and I refused to rejoice in her talent. (My husband wanted to buy me a sewing machine early in our marriage, but I convinced him that a glue gun would do. If his pants cuff droops when he leaves for work, I run for the stapler.) To rejoice honestly in one another's achievements, our *hearts* must become unselfish and Christlike. Why is this such a struggle? Is a Christlike attitude of joy and rejoicing for others possible for us?

Neill Foote Marriott is a homemaker who received her bachelor of arts degree from Southern Methodist University. A convert of twenty-five years, she serves as stake Relief Society president. Neill and her husband, David C. Marriott, are the parents of eleven children.

Patricia Holland outlined the problem: "Because of the increasing diversity of life styles for women of today, we seem even more uncertain and less secure with each other. We are not getting closer, but further away from that sense of community and sisterhood that has sustained and given us unique strength for generations. There seems to be an increase in our competitiveness and a decrease in our generosity with one another."[1]

We are mortal, and often our natural desire is to be selfish, to think of our wants and needs first. Though we want to become like the Savior, much of the time we are far from it. We worry, compare, compete, feel doubtful, and insecure as we fight a spiritual battle in a worldly arena. We are fearful when we don't "measure up" to others.

We should not take counsel from our fears. To resist their counsel, we must first identify those fears and self-doubts. Admit (even out loud, perhaps), "I am feeling afraid of Martha's opinion of me," or "I don't think I am as well-liked as Mary," or "I am afraid of failing in my new calling." Be honest with yourself, and you can begin to free yourself.

Once you have identified your fears, what then? You still haven't lost the twenty pounds, your husband heads for work with several staples glinting near his ankle, and your heart may still ache at comparisons. Willpower just isn't enough. You can't white-knuckle your anxious feelings into calm, confident thoughts. Doctrine and Covenants 6:36 tells us where to turn: "Look unto me in every thought; doubt not, fear not." We look to the Savior. We seek divine help. If we bring a broken heart and a contrite spirit to him, the Lord will make the changes in us that we cannot make in ourselves. We can't force our hearts to rejoice when we don't feel joyful—but Jesus Christ can take our feelings, if we offer them to him, and give us understanding, light, and a rejoicing love.

Consider this tender, encouraging invitation: "Abide in me, and I in you. As the branch cannot bear fruit of itself, except it abide in the vine; no more can ye, except ye abide in me. I am the vine, ye are the branches: He that abideth in me, and I in him, the same bringeth forth much fruit: for without me ye can do nothing" (John 15:4–5).

A few years ago I felt envy and ill-will toward a family member who is a very successful attorney and a good wife and mother. I did not rejoice in her law school honors and court-room success; I burned with resentment when she gained well deserved recognition. My discontent intensified after we had a disagreement about the legislation of women's rights. With her verbal skills, sharp intellect, and legal training, she took apart all my emotional reasoning and handily won the argument. Not only did I feel silly and uninformed but I probably was.

After our confrontation, I went in tears to Heavenly Father and poured out my feelings: "I don't like her, she doesn't respect my opinions—what am I going to do?" On and on I prayed, justifying my hurt feelings; finally I admitted to my loving Father in Heaven: "I think you probably want me to love her, but I don't think I even like her." As soon as I said those words, a certain ease came to my heart. Yes, that was the answer. He wanted me to love her and be glad for her successes—but how? I just plain didn't feel like it.

Then a clear, sweet understanding came. *I* might not love her, but Heavenly Father loves her. Could I come to feel about her the way he did? I felt a desire to love her, and with guidance from the Holy Ghost, my heart began to soften. I began to see who she really was. With spiritual eyes, I discovered an earnest, intelligent woman who wanted to give of herself and be a contributing part of our family, one who believed deeply in the rights of others, one who wanted to be accepted by me, one who cared about me.

As that light of understanding grew in me, love for her settled in my heart, and I began to rejoice in who she was and valued her as a human being and a daughter of God. This change of heart was and is a gift. Unclouded understanding and an attitude of rejoicing for others comes from our spiritual Father and our Savior through the Holy Ghost, for they can lift us out of our selfishness to rejoice in others as they do. At those times, I find I can lift and love others with more generous support, and when this happens, I feel connected and bonded to the one with whom I am sharing my acceptance and joy.

All this may sound improbable—to rid our hearts of envy and fill them with rejoicing in one another's achievements—but ultimately it is a matter of desire. Do we *want* to have such a heart? We can, but we must yearn for it and ask, as in Carol Lynn Pearson's simple but eloquent poem "The Uses of Prayer."

> Heaven
> Holds out the blessing
> Like a bright
> Ripe fruit,
> Only waiting
> For us to ask it:
>
> Our words
> Weave the basket.[2]

Our own secret prayers will open our hearts, enabling us to receive this gift: to understand and love as God loves. Let me share with you what works for me in praying.

First, I go into a quiet room and lock the door behind me. In my home are several little people who like to come into the room and watch me pray. While I do believe in being an example to my children, this young, solemn audience can be comical and distracting, so I lock the door and then don't worry about being interrupted. Next, I kneel down. For me, kneeling is important. Choosing to act in meekness opens the way for the Holy Ghost to influence my attitude.

I then pray out loud. I find that when I pray silently, I communicate clearly for a while and then I lapse into telling Heavenly Father such things as the price of lettuce. When I pray out loud, I stay focused. My prayers begin with what I suppose you could call a private testimony meeting, in which I share with my Heavenly Father all I know and love about him. As I do so, my weaknesses become very clear. I am acutely aware of my need for a Redeemer. I thank him for listening and simply pour out the feelings of my heart, fears, doubts, hopes, needs, failings, and gratitude.

My faith is stronger after these special prayers. I am sometimes instructed just by the thoughts I hear myself praying out loud, and I often feel as though a thick, soft, warm shawl has been gently placed around me. The feeling around me is tender, comforting, soft, reassuring, and warm. Sometimes my spirit feels filled with light, and then I see more clearly what Heavenly Father wants me to do or I understand another's feelings and needs correctly. Little by little, through prayer, I am gaining light and feeling nearer to my Father in Heaven.

Doctrine and Covenants 50:24 says, "That which is of God is light; and he that receiveth light, and continueth in God, receiveth more light." Prayer is surely the first step to receiving more light; and for me the next essential step is scripture study. The scriptures can powerfully illuminate our daily lives. They throw light on our individual circumstances. Through them, the Lord can help us fulfill our duties and give strength, hope, and direction. When we read hungering for help, we get help.

Twelve years ago I was called as Young Women president in my ward. The circumstances were not ideal. My husband was bishop of a University of Utah singles ward, I was expecting our seventh child, and our oldest was ten years old. At that time, the Young Women president was both the teacher and the adviser for the Laurel class. I had thirteen Laurels who were not particularly pleased with me or each other.

David was a wonderful bishop, and I was glad, but I compared my success rate with his and felt like a failure. Every Sunday I herded my children home after a trying Laurel lesson and then bawled. I used up a whole bottle of Visine that year trying to make my eyes look okay. My well of confidence and spirituality was dry, and I didn't see any fresh springs nearby.

One day I read in 1 Nephi 4:1: "Let us be faithful in keeping the commandments of the Lord; for behold he is mightier than all the earth, then why not mightier than Laban and his fifty, yea, or even than his tens of thousands?" I felt light and truth sink into my heart as I applied this blessed scripture to myself, "Neill, if the Lord *is* mightier than all the earth, then why not mightier than your discouragement and ineffectiveness?"

On my knees I presented the whole heavy burden, asking for some of his strength and wisdom. I trusted the scriptures. James 1:5–6 spoke to me: "If any of you lack wisdom, let him ask of God . . . and it shall be given him. But let him ask in faith." I felt reassured, and small moments of insight started coming. I could picture Christ reaching out to Jill, to Pam, to each of them—even to Lisa, who refused to attend. I knew that were Christ here, he would testify of Heavenly Father's love for each girl and his plan of salvation. Here was something I could do—in a personal visit bear my testimony to each individual Laurel. This simple idea found in prayer and scriptures resulted in a treasury of friendships, created by the power of the Holy Ghost that was present when we met one on one. Lisa never did come to a meeting or activity, nor did she ever indicate that she believed me when I bore my testimony in my monthly visits. Finally she moved, and we lost touch. Then, six years later, an invitation arrived to her temple wedding. I was thrilled for her and grateful she remembered me. After the ceremony she whispered to me, "You are one of the reasons I'm here today." Deeply moved, I knew it was the Lord who had used a stumbling Laurel teacher to speak the truth of his love to this girl.

Heavenly Father has a plan and a purpose for each of us. We are all "under heaven," as we are told in Ecclesiastes 3:1: "To everything there is a season, and a time to every purpose under the heaven." Heavenly Father knows our hearts and our gifts. When we look about and see others achieving but feel that we are not, then we must remind ourselves that we each have a purpose—and find through prayer and scripture study a way to rejoice in our own worth and the worth of others.

Sometimes life gets heavy and difficult, and we struggle to keep going. One of my favorite scriptures is Romans 8:28: "All things work together for good to them that love God." *All* things. This verse doesn't say, "All things, except disease, work together for good," or "All things, except being single," or "All things, except a less-active spouse," or "All things except financial ruin." It says *all* things. It doesn't say all things *are* good; it says they *work together* for good. For whom? For those who love God.

In our quest to see one another as God sees us, I suggest that we first love God. Then we will feel about one another more as he feels; we will grow in understanding one another, and our delight in each other's achievements will be a natural impulse. Our righteous desires to rejoice in others' achievements can bring greater goodness to this earth. In acknowledging the good we see in others, we become agents of a warmer, steadier, kinder sisterhood, the carriers of goodwill.

I know that I am powerless to create these rejoicings by myself. Mosiah 4:5 says a knowledge of God's goodness awakens us to a sense of our nothingness. Helaman 12:7 exclaims, "How great is the nothingness of men." We are at present in a fallen state, but a healing power is always available to empower us. The atonement of Jesus Christ is that power. Only his atonement can heal the wounds in our heart, the sins in our past, the fears for our future so that we may return home, rejoicing in one another's achievements to live God's life, eternally.

NOTES

1. Patricia T. Holland, "With Your Face to the Son," *BYU Today,* June 1987, 35.

2. Carol Lynn Pearson, "The Uses of Prayer," *The Search* (Provo, Utah: Trilogy Arts Publication, 1970), 31.

BETWEEN TWELVE AND TWENTY: A TIME OF CHANGE

VIRGINIA H. PEARCE

Have you ever wondered at how long your fifteen-year-old talks on the telephone, or the amount of time per week she spends in front of the mirror, or the number of outfits she takes from the closet before she decides what to wear? Perhaps you have watched a mother shudder as her teenaged son slouches into church with a new and bizarre haircut. What is happening to these usually reasonable and predictable children? In a simple phrase: they are hard at work. Their behaviors are all part of the process of becoming an adult.

Think about times of accelerated change in your own life experience. Remember those first few weeks on a new job and your feelings of confusion and inadequacy? Or remember a mission or a move and how it felt to suddenly have no identity—the strange feeling that no one knew your history. Adolescence is also a time of accelerated change.

RELOCATION: A TIME OF CHANGE

I always feel a sense of adventure and excitement when I arrive in a new home, neighborhood, and city. At the same time, I have feelings of insecurity—and dozens of questions:

Virginia H. Pearce serves as first counselor in the Young Women General Presidency. She received a master's degree in social work from the University of Utah. She and her husband, Dr. James R. Pearce, are the parents of six and the grandparents of seven.

What will be my new routine? Where and how will I shop, bank, go walking, get to know my neighbors? Will I find new friends? Does this neighborhood have new rules—most likely unwritten and unspoken—that I may trespass upon before I figure them out? Why do I feel almost invisible much of the time? And what is this kind of sick feeling in the pit of my stomach that seems to come and go? Is there someone I can find to ask all of these stupid questions—someone who knows the territory and will help me read the clues about how to talk, act, and do what I need to do?

Over and over again I don't even recognize myself. I feel timid about things that used to seem easy. I doubt my abilities and even past successes. I don't know what to expect from one day to the next. Similarly, the new administrative assistant in our office, who is new to Utah, said to me one day after a week of fairly violent weather, "Is this a normal spring?" I didn't know. I've been here so long that I do little more than watch the weather report and alter my day-to-day plans accordingly. But the weather in Salt Lake is just one of the things that Susan is trying to arrange into a predictable pattern as she adapts to all sorts of change.

Besides the loss of predictable patterns in the world, a move seems to precipitate more emotional ups and downs. One day in a new neighborhood I think, This is the best place I've ever lived. The next day I may be seized with despondency and dread of the future. Any emotional evenness I may have had gives way while I adjust and grow.

A friend of mine recently began a very intimidating new job. At the same time, she was building a new home and moving into a new neighborhood. I asked one day, "How's it going?" and she replied, "I am so sick of thinking about myself!" That is what change does to you. Initially you have to think about yourself a lot. I believe that this kind of egocentricity may have been what drove Enos in the Book of Mormon to desperate and intense prayer. He was experiencing a jolting change as he began his ministry as a prophet. His first concerns were totally egocentric—his own sins and weaknesses. Only after he received personal reassurance and forgiveness did he move on to the concerns of others (see Jacob 7:27–Enos 1).

After we have moved to a new home, what helps us progress beyond discomfort and egocentricity to a place of enlarged perspective and permanent growth? Mostly time. Simply being patient. We have learned from previous experiences that in time things will right themselves. Meanwhile, people who are not critical, who make us feel safe, and who invite us to ask all those "dumb questions" make adjustment a little less painful. A calling to serve in a new ward or branch may restore self-confidence, just when we are doubting our abilities. And watching people who are successfully navigating can provide clues to appropriate local behavior. In time we will become a comfortable and unself-conscious "local."

ADOLESCENCE: A TIME OF CHANGE

Adolescence is an even more prolonged time of dramatic and pervasive change. Remembering some of the feelings and tasks of moving to a new home will enlarge our understanding of young people's behavior. Adolescence is, by definition, a time of intense and profound change. Between the ages of twelve and twenty, a child becomes an adult. The physical changes alone are immense. Height and weight change dramatically. Hormonal changes set in motion processes that literally create a new person, both physically and emotionally.

The structure of life also changes for the adolescent. The elementary schoolteacher who assumed a presence much like a parent is replaced by seven junior high or high school teachers who no longer have the time or mandate to assume much personal responsibility for individual students. At a time of increasing choices, both academic and extracurricular, teens also have greater access to friends who live outside their immediate neighborhoods.

Parents often feel apprehensive when a child enters adolescence. In our industrialized society, adolescents are not viewed as assets to the family business as they were in more rural, agrarian times. More often, parents expect that the child will become a financial and emotional drain on the family. Community rhetoric echoes family anxiety. Young people are seen not as a resource to the community but as a potential threat, requiring extra resources.

Adult rhetoric concerning teens moves on a continuum from good-humored but negative jokes to actual fear. As that occurs, adults tend to distance themselves from and isolate the adolescent. Furthermore, because the individual stakes are high, adults unwittingly communicate fear, rather than faith, in the future of the emerging adult.

THE WORK OF ADOLESCENCE

Now think again of what it's like to move. Recall those feelings of disorientation, loneliness, isolation, loss of identity, confusion about newly required behaviors, inadequacy, excitement and adventurousness, lack of predictability, need for reassurance and acceptance, accelerated ups and downs, egocentricity, and self-doubt. Could they accurately describe the feelings of a normal, healthy, growing adolescent?

Add to those feelings a partial list of the massive work that will be done within a few years—the questions that will have to be answered before the unique new adult individual emerges—and our respect increases. The work of adolescence can be seen as the formation of individual identity—answering the question, Who am I? Included in this question are many others. There are gender questions (What does it mean to be male/female?), issues of attachments and belonging (How do I fit in with peer group/family/church structure/neighborhood? How do I make new friends? Will I ever have a boyfriend/girlfriend?), concerns about competence and skills (What do I know? What can I do? Can I contribute anything useful to anyone else? What am I capable of in the future?). In addition, the work of adolescence involves choices with *lifelong* consequences (Now that I know I don't have to be just like my mother/father, what are my choices? Who helps me figure out what options are available? What do I believe? What do I do about what I believe?) and difficult questions of validation (How do I know if I'm doing okay? What do siblings, friends, parents, teachers, and other adults think of me?).

WHAT CAN WE DO TO BE HELPFUL?

When we understand the feelings, it's easy to see that the very same things that are helpful during a geographic move can help an adolescent. First is time. Unlike adults, a fifteen-year-old has much less experience to help her or him know about time and the magic it can work. Therefore, it becomes even more important that adults communicate to the teen their own patience and faith in the process of time.

Strangely enough, helpful behavior, especially this faith in the process, is often very difficult for parents to provide for their own children. Often, we can be of the greatest help to other people's children. Wouldn't you be grateful to a wonderful adult who befriended your son or daughter, who made that child so new to adulthood feel safe enough to ask "dumb questions"? An adult can reassure with positive and respectful language, can model appropriate adult behavior with warmth and concern. Adults can help an adolescent explore new interests and opportunities, build new skills, and strengthen an emerging new identity. An adult can work alongside the young person, helping him or her to experience new feelings of competence.

I recently asked some young people to talk about the adults in their lives. I wanted to know some of the specific attitudes and actions that they perceived as helpful:

"I love it when adults in my ward call me by my first name—not 'Little Johnson'!"

133

"I love working with my stepdad. He's great at fixing things, and I've learned how to do a lot of that stuff."

"The guy I home teach with is really cool. He hired me to do his yardwork."

"There's this really old guy in our neighborhood. He always asks me about my dates."

"I like it when adults ask me for my opinion and then don't just try to shoot it down."

Your personal emotional comfort with yourself is of real help to an adolescent. Just knowing people who have success-fully negotiated adolescence and have become healthy adults is of great value in the chaotic climate of change. Ask the young people you know and care about what would be help-ful to them. You may be surprised that much of what you are already doing is significant in their lives. I have often heard Sister Janette Hales Beckham, Young Women General President, say, "When we talk about young people and their challenges, I feel anxious. When we listen to young people, I feel encouraged." I agree with her. Our Latter-day Saint youth, actively engaged in the process of change between twelve and twenty, both need and deserve our admiration and trust.

OF DIFFERENT FAITHS

PAMELA J. ATKINSON

I came to Salt Lake City eight years ago from the Northwest to work as an administrator of patient services at LDS Hospital. I had been recruited by Intermountain Health Care. My friends and family had tried to caution me: "You are going where?" "Well, Salt Lake City," I said. "But why? What an odd place. There are Mormons there." "There are?" I hadn't known. "Yeah, and they're really weird." The people I had seen during my interview trip seemed quite normal, but I promised my family I'd stay on the lookout.

When my daughter and I first arrived, I bought a house in Bountiful, mainly because daffodils were in bloom there and I was longing for flowers. I was recently divorced and found my new neighbors very friendly and warm—just great people. My youngest daughter was living with me; the older two were at college. Our neighbors invited us to meals. They invited us to church. But a lot of my newly met non-LDS friends warned, "Just watch out, Pamela. They only want you to convert you." After a while, because I didn't want to attend church or go to every ward social and fireside with them, I found some of my neighbors didn't really have much more to do with me. I was puzzled. I was still open to friendships; I just didn't want to attend church with them because I was going to my own. Then

Pamela J. Atkinson is vice president of Mission Services for Intermountain Health Care. She is actively involved in community work with homeless and low-income families and individuals. She has three children: Sally, Roger, and Heather. Pamela is an elder in the First Presbyterian Church in Salt Lake City.

it dawned on me one day that perhaps my daughter and I weren't seen as Christians. I recalled my daughter's excitement over her first friend at her new elementary school. She happily talked about her every evening when I arrived home, but one day during the second week, I found her at home crying. It seems that the new friend's mother had found out we weren't Latter-day Saints and had told her daughter the two girls could no longer be friends. We felt stunned. Was there something wrong with us?

When some family members came to Utah for a visit, I took them to Bountiful's lovely Mueller Park for a picnic. We opened a bottle of wine and sipped a glass with our meal. Other picnickers all must have been LDS, because they began whispering, some turning to face away from us, and others pointing at us. Uncomfortable, we finally packed up and left. Later the little eight-year-old girl who lived next door to us naively expressed the mixed message we were sensing: "You know, you two aren't too bad considering you're not LDS." Aha, we thought. That's it.

By the time my daughter was thirteen, she had a number of close LDS friends and was attending some of their activities. At home one evening, when I was drinking a glass of wine, I noticed her watching me. "What are you looking at me like that for?" I asked. Her answer was full of piety: "You'll never get to the celestial kingdom if you act like that." At the time, I didn't know what the celestial kingdom was. I have since learned. I have even learned that the angel on the temple is not Gabriel but Moroni!

Over the years, I have also gratefully come to know Latter-day Saints who did not treat non-Latter-day Saints as morally inferior or less than Christian. Non-Latter-day Saints in Utah have a great need to be liked for who they are, not just as possible LDS converts. Both Latter-day Saints and non-Latter-day Saints need to remember that our lives may be the only scriptures that some people read. What I've learned from my LDS friends, I've learned from their lives, their caring, their reaching out, their love of me as a human being.

Just a few years ago, I was housebound and on crutches after knee surgery. A Relief Society president called to see how I was managing and in no time at all had organized the women in my neighborhood. Every day gracious neighbors brought in meals; it was terrific. Perhaps the greatest statement of personal generosity came from my kitty-corner neighbor Liz, who called to ask, "How are you doing?" I said, "Well, right now I'm struggling." When she asked why, I explained, "Oh, I'm trying to make a pot of tea. Have you ever tried to make a pot of tea on crutches?" To my surprise she said, "I've never made a pot of tea, but I'll come over and you can tell me how." I thought that was terrific. In Moroni 7:47 you can read, "But charity is the pure love of Christ." That's what I felt with these LDS friends—they were really reaching out to me in my need at that time. I will always be grateful for them.

I've searched diligently for what I call "safe people"—those with whom I can share a dialogue about their Latter-day Saint faith and beliefs, who aren't going to try to convert me but just help me to understand. I think of such people as my tremendous friends Colleen and Neal Maxwell. I can say to my non-LDS friends, "Hey, the Maxwells like me for who I am, not necessarily as a possible convert—although I'm sure they would love to have me join their church. But they like me for who I am." Such acceptance gives me a great feeling.

Perhaps our charity could extend to a genuine interest in what other people believe. Sometimes on Monday mornings, my coworkers chat about the priesthood, about Relief Society, about their wards and bishops. But nobody asks me what went on at my Presbyterian church. I find myself thinking, Gosh, I wish somebody would say, "Hey, what happened at your church, Pamela?" My non-LDS friends might, but my LDS colleagues and friends are so full of their own thoughts because they've had such great Sundays that they don't think to ask what other people might have done on the weekend.

One feeling we hold in common is our love of Jesus Christ and the Old and the New Testaments. We are all God's children. I believe that Christ lived on earth and died for my sins as well as yours. I believe we can be saved through accepting Christ as our personal Savior. I believe that I will be judged on my whole life—my relationship with other people, my faith, and my actions. I wonder which of my beliefs makes me less of a Christian than some of my LDS friends. A lot of my non-LDS friends believe that Latter-day Saints have a different God and a different Jesus Christ, but discussions with my LDS friends have convinced me otherwise. Many of our beliefs are the same, yet at times, I sense that some LDS people feel that what I believe is of no consequence. That hurts.

It says in Alma 1:30, "Therefore they were liberal to all, both old and young, both bond and free, both male and female, whether out of the church or in the church." I respect that verse. As one of twenty-four elected elders, male and female in the Presbyterian Church, I am responsible for mission services and community outreach. Elders are elected by the congregation for three years' service, and then they usually have some time off before being elected to serve again. My current assignment is to help our church members reach out to the community by working with homeless and low-income people. We arrange for the youth to do home repair and yardwork for older people and to make sandwiches, serve dinner, and assist in other ways at the Salvation Army and the homeless shelter. We also help needy people in our church neighborhood. I raise and budget funds for homeless people who come by for food, for gasoline vouchers, and other needs. Along with the other twenty-three elders, I'm also responsible for spiritual growth of the church.

We should never forget that reaching out and caring for someone can make a great deal of difference in that person's life. Reach out to your non-LDS friends and neighbors and discover how your life can be enriched as mine has been because of my LDS friends. A few months ago, I walked in a little late to a meeting at the hospital. The only woman in a group of LDS men, I listened to talk about the LDS Church this and the LDS Church that. Finally somebody said, "Oops, sorry, Pamela. We forgot." And I said, "Oh, that's quite all right. We're all elders here." I'm grateful we knew each other well enough to share that joke.

Jesus said to love the Lord your God with all your heart and with all your soul and with all your mind. This is the first and greatest commandment. And the second is like unto it, love your neighbor as yourself (see Matthew 22:37–39). We are all neighbors, whether of the LDS faith or any other, and should be reaching out to each other in love.

NEW WAYS TO TEACH AND LEARN: CARING AND CONNECTING

BEVERLY B. ZIMMERMAN

One of my favorite comic strips is "Calvin and Hobbes." In one sequence, Calvin appears in nine different poses: driven with a herd of cattle, bottled like juice on a cannery assembly line, running circles in a squirrel cage, working on a chain gang, walking like a robot, squawking senseless phrases on a parrot perch, jumping with fright in a cemetery, being driven as a square peg into a round hole, and flapping around like a fish out of water.[1] In the final frame, Calvin and Hobbes head down the hill in their wagon. Calvin says, "Boy, am I glad to see *you,* Hobbes!" And Hobbes replies, "Another typical school day?" In this cartoon, artist Bill Watterson provides a clever commentary on how Calvin—and many of us—would characterize our educational experiences.

South American philosopher Paulo Freire uses the metaphor of banking to characterize a view of education not unlike Calvin's.[2] Freire criticizes teachers who see their role as depositing information into students' minds, and students who simply store those deposits. According to Freire, in this manner of learning, teachers first study a subject and prepare lectures and lesson plans in the privacy of their offices; second,

---

Beverly Burrup Zimmerman, assistant professor of English at Brigham Young University, holds a Ph.D. in instructional science. She and her husband, Scott Zimmerman, have seven children and one grandchild. She has served as a stake Relief Society president in her Orem, Utah, stake.

they expound about the subject to their students; and third, students faithfully write down what the teachers say.

As passive recipients, students never experience the subject. Rather they memorize what the teacher tells them and then repeat the information back on examinations. Thus, students see the result of a teacher's thinking but never experience the teacher's learning process. Teachers talk, and students listen. Teachers deposit ideas into the students' notebooks, and students store those deposits.

Unfortunately, this approach is all too common in schools, church settings, and other learning situations. Teachers assume they can transmit or deliver ideas from their own minds or from a text to students without ever asking students to interpret those ideas or to interact with the teacher. As a result, students doubt their ability to discover or create knowledge for themselves. Moreover, emphasizing *what* students learn (the content of a course) over *how* students learn (the process by which they learn) can lead to teachers like one I know who said point-blank: "I have been certified by the General Authorities to teach at BYU. When students have been certified, then I will entertain their ideas." Or, it may produce such teachers as the one I observed responding to a student: "If you had read the text, you wouldn't ask such a question."

During my training to become an instructional designer, I became interested in the current heated educational debate over appropriate metaphors for teaching and learning. Some of the most interesting thinking comes from Mary Field Belenky and other women researchers. In *Women's Ways of Knowing: The Development of Self, Voice, and Mind,* Belenky and her colleagues point out that psychological studies of wealthy male college students form the basis for our current theories of learning. Thus, many of our assumptions about education, Belenky argues, are biased because (1) few women have participated in educational studies or conducted them and

141

(2) when women have participated, the results have been analyzed using conclusions drawn from the study of men.[3]

Belenky's group interviewed 135 women from all walks of life: working women, women in the home, educated women, and women on welfare. Whereas the earlier studies of men had shown learners preferred independence, autonomy, and competition, the women Belenky studied preferred interdependence, nurturance, and cooperation. Thus, Belenky and others would like to replace the metaphors of banking and hierarchy with the metaphor of a web or a net whereby teachers and students connect with each other on equal terms and where students cooperate rather than compete with each other.

This model allows information to flow not only from the teacher to the students but from the students to the teacher. Connected teachers and students become partners who both engage in the learning process and discuss their insights. Thus, as connected teachers and students think and talk together, their roles merge—students become teachers and teachers become students.

Furthermore, Belenky found learners develop their own knowledge when teachers "emphasize connection over separation, understanding and acceptance over assessment, and collaboration over debate; if [teachers] accord respect to and allow time for the knowledge that emerges from firsthand experience; [and] if instead of imposing their own expectations and arbitrary requirements, they encourage students to evolve their own patterns of work based on the problems they are pursuing."[4]

As part of my dissertation research, I observed a male teacher who had implemented in his college writing classes Belenky's connected, supportive, collaborative classroom model. Later I attempted to adopt those same metaphors in my own classroom, in my church calling, and in my home.

I now teach technical writing at Brigham Young University. Establishing a caring and supportive classroom while still providing a rigorous course is not easy because most of my students are male upper-division science and engineering students, used to the lecture method of teaching.

The first essential step is to learn every student's name and to ask them to learn each other's names. That allows for more interactive class discussions. And I find that I genuinely respect my students' opinions; their many years of experience with textbooks has already prepared them to recognize good writing. They can usually describe what they like and dislike about the samples of resumes, letters, instruction manuals, and product specifications I give them. I also include collaborative assignments, small group discussions of each other's work, and after every writing assignment, I allot class time for students to comment on how they solved problems that arose and what they learned from the assignment.

I also discuss my own writing with students: I show them red marks by numerous editors and I describe some of the decisions (wise and otherwise) I've made in writing for a specific audience, purpose, or situation. At first, I worried that by seeing my mistakes, students would question my expertise in teaching the course. What I found was just the opposite. As one student told me: "I have to be honest and say that my first response to the other students' comments on my paper was anger. I kept thinking, He had no idea how hard I worked on this paper! Then I remembered the day you showed us all the changes you had to make on one of your computer manuals. You said it's hard to take criticism but it helped you see holes in your work. So I cooled down a bit and looked at his responses objectively."

Changing my teaching style has made me more flexible and more focused on teaching students and less on teaching subject matter. I've had a harder time using connected teaching in my Church calling as a stake Relief Society president. Our training from the Relief Society General Board to "Think, Pair, Share" certainly encourages connections, but unfortunately I

most often see the banking metaphor in Relief Society meetings—teachers talk and students listen. The only one who
really learns is the teacher.

Three years ago, we changed our stake women's conference from an "Education Week" format in which women sat in
classes and listened to experts to one in which the women in
the stake shared their own stories. Over the course of three
years, we have heard from many fine women in our stake—
women who have sacrificed and suffered, who have been chal-
lenged by death, divorce, or personal illness, who have turned
to the Lord for strength. This shared sisterhood has enabled
many sisters to face and accept their own struggles.
Unfortunately, our attempts at learning through connection
have not always been understood by some who fear a woman's need for sharing may lead to "gossip" or who consider a
discussion of challenges to be negative.

I have had an even harder time applying the metaphor of
caring and connection in my own home. Because I'm stubborn,
it's taken me a while to learn that preaching isn't teaching.
Connected teaching means I must let go of the need to control
or manipulate my husband and our children. As a result, our
family home evenings have become less formal. Some of the
best teaching happens while we're playing games or just sharing the day's experiences. When I saw a need to encourage my
children to get along better, for example, instead of preaching
about being tolerant, we took a personality test and discovered
that personality differences are fun. Being more tolerant and
accepting of each other was a natural outcome.

Slowly, I'm discovering that sometimes the best way to
teach in the home is just to listen. Recently, my daughter was
called as president of her Mia Maid class and needed to choose
her counselors. When she asked for my advice, my first
impulse was to tell her which girls I thought would make good
counselors. Instead, I asked her what she had done so far in
trying to decide and how she felt about it. As she explained to

me how she had prayed about each girl in her class and felt good about certain names, she realized she had already received her answer.

It's never easy to make changes, but my efforts to change my teaching style have brought some unexpected bonuses. As I've struggled to share my writing with my students, I've discovered areas where I can improve. Hearing other women share their struggles has given me courage to better accept and handle my own. By listening to my children, I have come to understand myself.

In the end, by caring, by sharing, by listening, both students and teachers are better taught. I have learned much more, and I have become a better teacher, leader, and parent as I've learned to value my own—and others'—experiences. Shouldn't a few frames of caring and connection be worked into the Calvin and Hobbes cartoon? Teaching and learning would be the better for it. Nel Noddings expressed it well when she stated: "It is time for the voice of the mother to be heard in education."[5]

NOTES

1. Distributed by Universal Press Syndicate, 14 Mar. 1993.

2. Paulo Freire, "The 'Banking' Concept of Education," in *A Community of Voices: Reading and Writing in the Disciplines,* ed. Toby Fulwiler and Arthur W. Biddle (New York: MacMillan, 1992), 892–903.

3. Mary Field Belenky et al., *Women's Ways of Knowing: The Development of Self, Voice, and Mind* (New York: Basic Books, 1986).

4. Ibid., 229.

5. Nel Noddings, *Caring, a Feminine Approach to Ethics and Moral Education* (Berkeley: University of California Press, 1984), 200.

IN SEARCH OF SPIRIT:
LIFE WRITINGS OF
LATTER-DAY SAINT WOMEN

MAUREEN URSENBACH BEECHER

*A journal entry is a piece saved from the fabric of a
woman's day. Ragged, incomplete, misshapen—only its
color and pattern are left to show how it fits with its mates.*

And now that I have written this long, disconnected rambling remembrances of the past," wrote Mormon pioneer Margaret Judd Clawson in the late nineteenth century, "I Scarsly know what to do with it For who Can be interested in the little things of [the] Common, everyday life of another?"[1]

I, for one, and my colleagues are interested. Since the birth some thirty years ago of the study of women's history, we have valued every such text for the richness of its details: its little things. From just such rambling remembrances as those of Margaret Clawson, we have been able to extract the details which, analyzed and synthesized, allow us to construct and illustrate a history of the Latter-day Saint past, female.

As I have worked in archive collections abstracting an over-all picture, however, I have realized that my joy was not in the

Maureen Ursenbach Beecher is professor of English and an associate at the Joseph Fielding Smith Institute for Church History at Brigham Young University. A former missionary to Switzerland and a ward Relief Society president, she lives in Salt Lake City with her teenaged children.

generalizations I could draw but in each life I was reading. Something in the handwritten, sometimes penciled, often naive, misspelled, uncluttered account each woman gave of herself drew me in and held me fast. I would find the single detail or particular description I needed for my historical analysis; then, guilt nudging at my elbow to move to other sources, I would read on, and on, and on. Each writer, whom I viewed first as informant, became by stages an individual, a woman, an acquaintance, my friend, my sister. The historical data became a by-product of what is now to me a much more satisfying search: the life writings of Latter-day Saint women, a literature of its own. Richard Cracroft and Neal Lambert, in their anthology *A Believing People,* introduced me to Mary Goble Pay's description of her family's arrival in Utah with the handcart companies: "We arrived in Salt Lake City nine o'clock at night the 11th of December 1856. Three out of four that were living were frozen. My mother was dead in the wagon.

"Bishop Hardy had us taken to a home in his ward and the brethren and the sisters brought us plenty of food. We had to be careful and not eat too much as it might kill us we were so hungry.

"Early next morning Bro. Brigham Young and a doctor came. The doctor's name was Williams. When Bro. Young came in he shook hands with us all. When he saw our condition—our feet frozen and our mother dead—tears rolled down his cheeks."[2]

The passage defies analysis by any of the criteria by which I was taught to recognize good writing. Simple sentences, or run-on, or fragmentary. Interjections. Dangling modifiers. Little words—only two with more than two syllables in the whole passage. But a Hopkins sonnet or a John Donne sermon has not the power to move me as has this honest piece so simply written. The literary canon must expand to allow it a place.

Our manuscript collections are rich with the life writings of ordinary Latter-day Saint women from our recent past. Brigham

Young University's Harold B. Lee Library, among other local repositories, has such gems packed away in Fiberdex boxes, often untouched from year to year. Not the written-for-publication works of famous women, these are either the daily jottings of mothers, wives, daughters, or the women's mature attempts to set their lives in order, to explain themselves not to the world but to their children and their children's children in the Puritan tradition of testimony bearing and lasting testament. In loose sheets or bound notebooks, they are as imperfect as the lives they represent, as incomplete as a peek through the keyhole, as unfinished as mortality.

As we broaden the literary canon to include these texts, we establish a corpus of the life writings of ordinary women. How do we then approach them critically? What principles can guide our reading? How do they reach us, these private pieces?

First there is the question of genre. Diaries—or journals—differ from autobiographies or memoirs or reminiscences. Let me use a homely metaphor to make some distinctions. Mary White was one of the West Texas quiltmakers interviewed by Patricia Cooper and Norma Bradley Buferd for their 1978 book, *The Quilters*. For Mary, quilting was a way to see the world: "You can't always change things. Sometimes you don't have no control over the way things go. Hail ruins the crops, or fire burns you out. And then you're given so much to work with in a life and you have to do the best you can with what you've got. That's what piecing is. The materials is passed on to you or is all you can afford to buy . . . that's what's given to you. Your fate. But the way you put them together is your business. You can put them in any order you like."[3]

The image works as well to explain not only the living of a life but also the writing of one. Each recorded moment, each diary entry, is a piece saved from the fabric of a woman's day. Ragged, incomplete, misshapen—only its color and its pattern are left to show how it fits with its mates. Like fabric scraps, a diary is a jumble of unconnected pieces tossed together into a box and pushed under the bed.

Years later, having survived the more demanding necessities of her life, a woman might eventually pull out her box of swatches or blocks and arrange them into a full quilt top. "You can put them in any order you like," Mary White said. Wedding Ring, Log Cabin, Windmill, Flying Geese, or Crazy Quilt—she would now create a thing of beauty in which every piece connected artistically and permanently to its neighbor and every block had its partner. Each piece that the collector still liked, that is, or would acknowledge as hers. That is an autobiography. Its intricacy or simplicity tells more about the woman at the time of its quilting than of the blocks at the time of their origin. It uses the stuff of the past merely as the raw material out of which the present is recreated.

Take Annie Clark Tanner, for example. You may know her as *A Mormon Mother* from her fine autobiography published by her son Obert in 1969.[4] From first to last, we have not the child Annie growing up, the girl Annie attending Brigham Young Academy, the young woman Annie marrying into polygamy, or the mother Annie rearing her children alone in Farmington. Instead each part is cut to shape and placed in the whole to reveal to the mature, reflecting Annie—and to the reader—the meaning of the contradictions in her life. In composing the autobiography, Annie drew on her collection of her diaries and letters, which, her son later told me, were destroyed. How sad. In the spaces between the diary and the autobiography, what might we learn of growth, of struggle, of developing self-awareness?

Then we might have of Annie what we do have of Rhoda Dykes Burgess, whose diary, as typed by her granddaughter, recently came to hand. Begin anywhere—it hardly matters. Try January 15, 1882, Pine Valley, Utah. "It is snowing very hard to day there has been no meeting nor Sunday school most of the men are away at work I am not well to day Eliza has been writing the young folks are having a sleigh ride oh how I miss my Dear Mother when I am sick."[5]

Then begin to trace the pieces. "Today's" snow will last for months, even though this is Pine Valley, not thirty miles from St. George—Utah's usual hot spot. The Burgesses have come down from their farm in Grass Valley, farther up the mountains, where the winter is even harder, to live until summer. It helps to have neighbors, especially in winter. In spring, Rhoda and George will again move their household the twelve miles north.

It is Sunday as Rhoda writes. Even so, the men are away at work. The men are usually away at work. "I am not well today" is a rare complaint for Rhoda, and a foreshadowing: in three weeks, she will bear her tenth child and sixth daughter. On the eve of the birth, Rhoda will write: "I have been cleaning washed and Ironed a littel the Children are home from school Geo is back from Grassvalley supper is over and the littel ones are in bed the snow is quite deep and the weather very cold I am so lonely to night and selfish enough to wish my Dear old Mother here with me."[6]

Anticipating the birth without "my Dear old Mother" is particularly trying; Dorcas Keeling Dykes (Grandma to the children, Ma to Rhoda) had been sick through most of December. The diary reads:

"Dec 12 the Children came from Grandmas this morning said she was sick so I hurried down found her in bed she said she was a littel better she had had a chill . . .

Dec 13 I have been sick all day . . . so I did not go down till evening found her much better she said she wanted her supper so we got it she ate hearty seemed to enjoy it

Dec 14 Ma is not so well to day has that old pain in her side

Dec 15 Ma is no better and yet she does not seem very sick her appetite is quite good and her mouth is all broke out with cold sores . . .

Dec 16 Ma sent word to me not to come down to day as she felt much better I am so glad . . .

Dec 17 I hurried down to Mas this morning found she had spit blood all night . . . I hope it is nothing serious I have seen her spit blood before this Brother Lloyd has just administered to her I do wish George was here—evening—Lord help us to say Thy will be done our Dear old Mother has passed away to a better world than this."

"The snow is falling on her grave today," Rhoda writes as she draws one day nearer her own passage through "the valley of the shadow of death" that was giving birth.

So, patch after patch, the quilt pieces jumble into Rhoda's box. Life. Raw life. Day by tedious day. "I have been piecing a flannel quilt and tearing carpet rags all day." The fabric of a woman's life.

But not always so heavy with responsibility. Take Lizzie Conrad, nearly nineteen and waiting for her true love to return, writing to her diary as though to a friend, and signaling with a squiggle each day a letter arrives from her Hyrum: "Little Journal I haven't written any in you for a long time I have neglected you and my mind is getting rusty. Sacred little book you will keep my secrets wont you."

The persona is innocence itself, springtime pregnant with promise but threatened by approaching summer: "21st of March [1894] This is my birthday. I am 19 years old. I ought to be a woman now. Oh what a responcibility. The oldest one of the family ought to be able to take the place of ma. [Lizzie's mother will give birth next month.] Hyrum is coming home, am I happy or sorry? I am glad he is coming home, but sorry I have not been a better girl and proven my self more worthy of him. . . . I was such a child when he went away and a very thoughtless girl and Hyrum the boy that he was, sent away to preache the Gospel, he will come home with a great deal of experience and a strong testimony of the truth. I wonder if I will ever be worthy of him."

151

Hyrum does return, and the diary, like the Velveteen Rabbit, is forgotten a while. A year passes.

"Well my little book it has been a long time since I've told you how I felt. I'd feel pretty well if I'd done right all the time but I have not. I thought at one time I had more trouble than any one, but the old saying is, that time is the great healer of all wounds, and he has partly healed mine. After having taken a fancy to the German lad his folks took it into their heads that it must not be so. They there fore decided to seperate us by the Atlantic Ocean, and thought that I would soon marry and their son would be saved but that scheme dident work. Hyrum and I felt the same as of old towards each other. His folks still treat me cool. He left for Scofield on the 15 of May to raise some money to pay of[f] his mission debt and of corse I am left alone again."[7]

The course of true love, et cetera, et cetera. But true true love it seldom is. For personal texts are the fictions we create to make our lives acceptable to ourselves. By omissions, by evasions, or by outright untruths, we reshape events to our liking. "I don't remember why I was lying here," observed a young friend on reading her own teenage diary, "but I know this is a lie."[8] Our memories are flawed—distorted—as people discover when they share their version of an event with that of a sibling or a spouse. But within every text is imbedded a deeper truth, a transcendent reality trying to emerge.

Before he allowed the Church historian to look at his diary, my grandfather carefully razored out small sections. More frequently we totally omit details which belie the persona we are trying to present. Spaces. Silences. Perhaps the most interesting part of the autobiographical record is what is left out and why. In my grandfather's case, notes were deleted after inclusion. Perhaps they reflected ill on another person; perhaps they spoke a truth which, in the days of post-Manifesto plural marriage, could be damaging to the Church; perhaps they simply contradicted the self he wished to portray. That another of my ancestors noted the birth of one of his children in the margin, as an afterthought, need not suggest that the birth meant little to him; it could as easily reflect his sense of what a man's journal ought to concern itself with.

Women, too, have been known to suppress parts of their records or even to destroy the entire record. More often what happens in a woman's world seems to her simply too mundane, too routine, too insignificant to warrant mention. The "dailiness" of a woman's life, Laurel Ulrich calls it; the ongoing "woman's work" that creates the core around which the household members build their lives; the "little things" Margaret Clawson deemed of no interest.

Emma Lorena Barrows Brown, called in the 1880s as president of the Wasatch Stake Relief Society, kept a lean diary of her activities. The few events and activities she considered worthy of mention are framed by the omission of the ones she did not deign to note. "At home," she would write, "at home and washed," "at home all day," "quilted a quilet raining," "at home ironed," "at home," summarizing for herself the demanding tasks of keeping house in rural Charleston, Utah. In contrast, Relief Society activities are spelled out in her 1878 entries:

"Sun 28 [July 1878] went to R Society Meeting [.] Meeting comenced at 9 Oclock Sister E R Snow & Zina Young spoke and gave ous some good instruction went to Sunday School then went to Bro Murdock to Dinner went to afternoon Meeting come home and got Supper then went to the Y[oung] L[adies'] Meeting Sis Snow Zina Young spoke had a good meeting."[9]

Whether the task of diary keeping became too onerous, the weather too unremittingly hot, or Emma Lorena simply unable to find significance in her activities, in August 1880 the life of the thirty-seven-year-old wife, mother, sister, and president is reflected in an even more sparse series:

"Thu 19 went on the hills back of our place Lizza came over

"Fri 20 started home on a load of hay
"Sat 21 at home
"Sun 22 at home Geo went after the Cows
"Mon 23 at home
"Tus 24 at home
"Wed 25 at home
"Thu 26 at home
"Fri 27 at home
"Sat 28 at home
"Sun 29 went to Meeting
"Mon 30 wash"

The columnar appearance of August's entries and the apparent sameness of her days may well have discouraged Emma Lorena. After three similarly brief September entries, she inscribed the date and day of the week along the margin and left six weeks' worth of empty spaces from "Fri 3 at home" to October 22. Then she noted, after a space of a word's length, "& Ethan came home." A similar hiatus commenced again November 11 and continued to December 14, when even the dates no longer appear. Empty pages represent January and February 1881, designating presumably the diarist's intent to summarize those months later. Then the passage of March through November is simply noted by month. September is the exception: "On the 23 of this month William Leonard Brown was Born." Whether pregnancy had been more than usually difficult, the summer more than usually hot, the work more than usually dreary, or the baby more than normally difficult, only Emma Lorena can know. For us it is left to ponder the silences, the spaces, and their meaning in the framework of the whole diary. Reading on, we feel relief when in November "Geo went to Provo to meet Sister Horn and Howard," and the Relief Society work resumes for President Brown. It is easier to deal with the positive statements than the negative spaces.

Margaret Judd Clawson, with whom this essay began, wrote in full and delightful detail of her young womanhood, of crossing the plains, of performing in the Salt Lake Theater, of young motherhood, of the social life that whirled around her family. But of the backstage romance and her marriage as second wife to Hiram Clawson, she writes only: "In 1852 I was sealed to Hiram B. Clawson by President Brigham Young and I have no cause to regret ever having taken that step For he has been a Kind, Considerate husband and a most indulgent Father to all of his Children." Four years later, when Margaret was four months pregnant with their son Rudger, Hiram married a third time. Her pain and that of Hiram's first wife, Ellen Spencer Clawson, are reflected in that woman's letter to her friend Ellen McGary in San Bernardino telling of the new marriage: "I think perhaps Margaret feels worse than I do for she was the last, and I suppose thought he would never get another, the same as I did."[10] In an autobiography written presumably for her children, Margaret did not share the anguish, the ache, the sorrow engendered by her marriage in polygamy. Nor perhaps could she acknowledge the seemingly illicit delight of being courted and won by a man already someone else's husband. In any case, in her reminiscence, as in so many LDS women's accounts, her soon-to-be husband is a shadow, a phantom, seldom named or seen.

Margaret's sister-wife Ellen, however, is freer in her letter—she knows, or thinks she knows, that her words will be kept private by one who will understand. After that third marriage, Ellen confides to her friend: "I feel as though it would do me good to write, for my heart is rather heavy. I never thought I could care again if Hiram got a dozen wives, but it seems as though my affections return with double force, now that I feel as if I had lost him but I expect he thinks as much of me as ever, only in a different way you know a new wife is a new thing, and I know it is impossible for him to feel any different towards her just at present, still it make[s] my heart ache to think I have not the same love, but I console myself with thinking it will subside into affection, the same as it is with me, for you know the honey-moon cannot always last at least if you dont know it now you will sometime perhaps."

Words tumble pell-mell from Ellen's pen, her grief revealed to her friend. Such intimate disclosure is rare in an autobiography and in most diaries. In deigning to read such a letter, we who seek to understand the burdens of the past count ourselves among the writer's confidants and assume with reverence an obligation of compassion and love. We, too, become sisters and friends.

Quilts, embroideries, tapestries—fabrics of women's lives, these personal narratives. Loosely woven or still on the loom, bobbins dangling, colors yet to be interwoven; or tightly bound and neatly finished, ends tucked in, seams hidden. Unique as the mind that conceived them, the hands that made them, they warm us, please our eye, delight our sensibilities, evoke our love. Let us not participate longer in the silencing of the voices of our sisters of past and present. Let us find their texts, read them, share them, and learn from them. In them we find ourselves.

NOTES

This essay is an excerpt from an article previously published in *BYU Studies* 34, no. 4 (1994–95), 14–45, and taken originally from the Alice Louise Reynolds Lecture, 17 Mar. 1994, Harold B. Lee Libraries, Brigham Young University, Provo, Utah.

1. Margaret Gay Judd Clawson, "Rambling Reminiscence of Margaret Gay Judd Clawson," holograph, Archives Division, Historical Department, The Church of Jesus Christ of Latter-day Saints, Salt Lake City; hereafter cited as LDS Church Archives. Courtesy of Jean Greenwood and Kathlene Fife Jackson, who transcribed the text. See also *Relief Society Magazine* 6 (1919): 257–62, 317–27, 391–400, 474–79; and excerpts in Gordon Irving, ed., "Teenage Pioneer: The Adventures of Margaret Judd Clawson," *New Era* 4 (May 1974): 44–50. BYU's Religious Studies Center is publishing the entire Clawson manuscript as prepared by Kathlene Fife Jackson in a volume edited by Claudine Foudray Gallacher.

2. Mary Goble Pay, "Death Strikes the Handcart Company," in *A Believing*

People: Literature of the Latter-day Saints, ed. Richard H. Cracroft and Neal E. Lambert (Provo, Utah: Brigham Young University Press, 1974), 107.

3. Patricia Cooper and Norma Bradley Buferd, *The Quilters: Women and Domestic Art* (Garden City, N.Y.: Doubleday, 1978), 20.

4. Annie Clark Tanner, *A Mormon Mother: An Autobiography by Annie Clark Tanner* (Salt Lake City: Tanner Trust Fund, University of Utah Library, 1969).

5. "The Journal of Rhoda Ann Dykes Burgess," typescript in possession of the author, courtesy of Lois Shepherd Beck and Jill Mulvay Derr.

6. Ibid., 6 Feb. 1882.

7. Mary Elizabeth Conrad Muhlestein, Diary, 1891–1900, holograph, Special Collections, Harold B. Lee Library, Brigham Young University, Provo, Utah. Muhlestein's diary, as edited by Amy Cutt Lopez, will shortly be published by BYU Religious Studies Center.

8. Amanda McPeck, conversation with the author, 15 Mar. 1994.

9. Emma Lorena Barrows Brown journal, holograph in possession of Jean Duke Howe.

10. Ellen Spencer Clawson to Ellen Pratt McGary, 4 November 1856, in S. George Ellsworth, *Dear Ellen: Two Mormon Women and Their Letters* (Salt Lake City: Tanner Trust Fund, University of Utah Library, 1974), 33.

RELIEF SOCIETY: SO WHAT?

MARJORIE DRAPER CONDER

Five years ago, while hurrying out the door to Relief Society one Sunday morning, I had a flash of inspiration for my lesson and ran back into the house to dash off a visual aid. During the lesson I listed some of the many voices that tell us there is always something more to do. Advertisers tell us we've got to try a new soft drink; the dentist thinks we should floss; our kids want the latest software. The list goes on and on. Sometimes even church can seem like a commandment-of-the-week club. To my Relief Society sisters I said, "After a while, you may just want to shut all the voices out. So I have a question for you. If you can't answer this question to your satisfaction, you don't have to do anything about anything we've said here today—and you don't have to feel guilty. You can just forget about it." I held up my hastily made cardboard visual aid that said, "SO WHAT?" Everybody laughed. But the question led to a productive discussion.

I have often asked myself this same question. In 1990, I was assigned to be in charge of the Relief Society sesquicentennial exhibit at the Church Museum. At first I was excited. Then I asked myself, "Relief Society, so what?" Why should we

Marjorie Draper Conder received her master's degree from the University of Utah and is a curator at the Museum of Church History and Art. She and her husband, Darrell Conder, have six children and nine grandchildren. Marjorie teaches Spiritual Living lessons in her ward Relief Society.

be spending sacred tithing money to put on an exhibit about the Relief Society?

To find an answer to that question, I first reviewed the history. In 1842, all of Nauvoo was focused on the construction of the Nauvoo Temple. Some women gave their churned butter to the workmen; some knitted socks and mittens. Sisters Mercy Fielding Thompson and Mary Fielding Smith collected pennies from as far away as England to buy nails and glass. Sarah Granger Kimball, only twenty-three but one of the wealthiest women in Nauvoo, was married to Hyrum Kimball, not a Church member. In her home lived "Miss Cook" who helped with domestic chores. Miss Cook had a great desire to help with the Nauvoo Temple but no resources. Sarah Kimball had resources but, with a new baby, little time. They combined their assets: Sarah provided fabric, needles, thread, and the warm parlor where Sister Cook and others met to sew shirts for the men constructing the temple.

As they sewed, the women discussed formalizing their association in some way. Apparently, however, no woman in this little sewing group had enough self-confidence to draft a constitution for the proposed group. So they asked Eliza R. Snow, the best-known writer in Nauvoo. Eliza took what she had written to Joseph Smith, who told her the constitution was the best he had ever seen and then added, "but this is not what you want. Tell the sisters their offering is accepted of the Lord, and He has something better for them."[1] Then he invited the sisters to meet with him in the upper story of his Red Brick Store the following Thursday.

I have heard that pleasantly familiar story many times. As with the Christmas story, I enjoy knowing what is coming next. In preparing the sesquicentennial exhibit, however, I asked myself, "What exactly was the something better?" What I found led me to a new understanding of what God intends for women in these latter days—the civil and religious empowerment of women in the Restoration.

159

Although Emma Smith, elected president at the first meeting, declared, "We are going to do something *extraordinary*,"[2] the women involved in that first Relief Society could not have guessed what this modest organization, begun as a sewing circle, would soon accomplish in Nauvoo, not to mention its future into the present. In the founding meeting, second counselor Sarah Cleveland said, "We design to act in the name of the Lord—to relieve the wants of the distressed, and do all the good we can."[3] After formally establishing themselves as the "Female Relief Society of Nauvoo," the twenty women in that initial group organized themselves two by two to survey the needs of the women of Nauvoo and do what they could to help. They called themselves the Necessity Committee. The name has changed, but what they were about has not. Of Nauvoo's nearly ten thousand residents at the time, most lived in desperate want in log cabins, shacks, and even shanties. We don't often think of Nauvoo as a frontier city of refugees and immigrants, but that is what it was. These women were also early activists. They even voted to boycott merchants who were cheating widows, hoping thus to combine their strength to safeguard sisters who were defenseless and economically oppressed.

Perhaps the most interesting Relief Society meeting ever was held a little over a month later, on 28 April 1842, again in the Red Brick Store. The Prophet Joseph, who attended some but not all of the meetings, was at this one. He preached to the women from 1 Corinthians 13 on charity as a particular gift of women. The apostle Paul's phrase "charity never faileth" (v. 8) eventually became the Relief Society motto. He told the women to be kind to their husbands and to love one another. What he said next, recorded in the meeting minutes, has often been misquoted. He said, "I now *turn the key to you* in the name of God and this Society shall rejoice and knowledge and intelligence shall flow down from this time. This is the beginning of better days to this Society."[4] Often he has been quoted as saying,

". . . as I turn the key in your behalf." But these statements are almost exact opposites. One is doing something, however nice, for somebody else. The other empowers women to act and to do for themselves in a way previously unheard of.

Perhaps the word *key* in this context has made some Church members uncomfortable. When we hear the word *key,* we generally think of priesthood; however, a key also symbolizes giving access to something you cannot do without a key. Your house key lets you (and not others) into your house. Your car key gives you access to your car. With this key the Prophet gave all women everywhere access to "better days." To the best of my knowledge, none of these nineteenth-century women ever claimed ordination to any priesthood office. They did, however, claim to have been empowered by what Joseph Smith did in that April 1842 Relief Society meeting in Nauvoo.

Later in the nineteenth century, Latter-day Saint women were charter members of both the National Council of Women and the International Council of Women. They were close personal friends of many leading women of their day, including Susan B. Anthony, who spoke in the Salt Lake Tabernacle in 1895. These LDS women, a tiny, tiny minority in the national and international councils of women, stated publicly in these forums that if a prophet of God had not turned a key to women, somehow empowering them, the women then gathered would be as powerless to move forward the righteous cause of women as women had been throughout history. In a general Relief Society conference held in 1945, President George Albert Smith said, "When the Prophet Joseph Smith turned the key for the emancipation of womankind, it was turned for all the world, and from generation to generation the number of women who can enjoy the blessings of religious liberty and civil liberty has been increasing."[5] We have all witnessed this literal unfolding, and it is part of our heritage through the Relief Society.

Another part of our Relief Society heritage is its role in

preparing women for temple covenants. At times, various brethren accompanied Joseph Smith to Relief Society meetings. Reynolds Cahoon, one of these men, stated: "This society is raised by the Lord to prepare us for the great blessings which are for us in the House of the Lord—in the Temple."[6] This statement was indeed remarkable for the 1840s. Before the founding of the Relief Society, no woman in Nauvoo expected to take part in any type of temple ordinance. We often assume that because the Saints were building a temple, everybody knew what would happen there. That is not so. Temple ordinances as we know them had not yet been revealed. In Kirtland, the temple had been used primarily as a meeting-house. The upstairs rooms housed the School of the Prophets. Even if the women had known about temple ordinances, they would not have expected to take part in them. They were women of their time and anticipated nothing more than they were used to.

Since Joseph Smith turned the key, women's social, political, and economic status has improved worldwide. Of even greater importance, the spiritual empowerment of women is central to our endowment as latter-day women of covenant. In July 1830, almost twelve years before the founding of the Relief Society, the Lord revealed the first openings of women's enlarged destiny. Among other things, he said in this revelation to Emma: "Thou shalt be ordained under [my servant Joseph's] hand to expound scriptures, and to exhort the church, according as it shall be given thee by my Spirit" (D&C 25:7). In 1830, it was very rare indeed for women to speak or take an active role in church. Most churches were still quoting Paul that women should be silent in church (see 1 Corinthians 14:34–35). Women did not expect public roles in any setting.

A watershed event in women's history was the Seneca Falls Convention, held in Seneca Falls, New York, in 1848, six years after the founding of the Relief Society.[7] The women and men who came together to this convention had been working for the abolition of slavery for many years. Eight years earlier, in 1840, an American delegation had traveled to England for an international antislavery convention. At that time in Europe, even more than in America, women were banned from virtually all public activity. Against custom, the American antislavery delegation included women. The convention officials, with great consternation, mulled over what to do with these Americans who so little respected "their place" as women. They finally decided to seat the women in the balcony behind a screen. Frederick Douglass, an influential black American, had the grace to sit with them. Perhaps only he fully grasped the implications of their situation. These American women, who had been fighting for the emancipation of Negro men, suddenly realized that their position was little better, except for their privileged economic circumstances.

That was in 1840. For eight long years, they muddled, uncertain what to do about their new awareness of the real status of women. I believe they were *unable* to do anything to move the cause of women forward at that time because a prophet had not yet turned a key to women everywhere. The most memorable event of the Seneca Falls Convention was a restatement of the Declaration of Independence to explicitly include women. "We hold these truths to be self-evident: that all men *and women* are created equal; that they are endowed by their Creator with certain inalienable rights," it began. Surprisingly, the most controversial issue was whether or not women should seek the vote. That issue almost split the convention.

Compare this group's timidity with Abigail Adams' bold request sixty-six years before. On 31 March 1776, she wrote to her husband John, away at the Second Continental Congress: "I long to hear that you have declared an independancy—and by the way in the new Code of Laws . . . I desire you would Remember the Ladies, and be more generous and favourable to them than your ancestors. . . . Remember all Men would be tyrants if they could. If perticuliar care and attention is not paid to the Laidies we are determined to foment a Rebelion, and will not hold ourselves bound by any Laws in which we have no voice, or Representation."8 Abigail was demanding the vote for women be written into the constitution of the new nation.

Abigail Adams was a witty, articulate, well-educated woman. George Washington, Benjamin Franklin, James Madison, and Thomas Jefferson were counted among her friends. Abigail was more forthright and courageous than the women of Seneca Falls, but the key had not yet been turned to women, and Abigail made no progress. John Adams this once (and the only time I know of, for John and Abigail are really a great American love story) penned a very condescending reply: "As to your extraordinary Code of Laws, I cannot but laugh. . . . Depend upon it, We know better than to repeal our Masculine systems."9

Contrast that with the remarkable gifts—both temporal and eternal—bestowed on women from God through a prophet in 1842. The temple and its blessings are central to the changing status of women as part of the Restoration. We do not know when the first females were endowed, but evidence suggests that it may have been within a couple of months of the founding of the Relief Society. Those first men and women to be endowed were looked upon by other Church members as holy and set apart—perhaps a view we need to restore. By the mid twentieth century, when I was a teenager, teachers and parents spoke to us of temples almost exclusively as places to get married. Few girls my age thought of the temple as a place to be set apart and empowered to serve in the kingdom. For me, that is one of the "so-whats" of studying our history: it reaffirms my testimony of the centrality of temples and covenants with Christ.

Because of their experiences, first with Relief Society and then in the temple, the women of Nauvoo understood that they were being given holy power as daughters of God to act and not just to be acted upon (see 2 Nephi 2:26). Virtually all of the adults who left Nauvoo to come West had been endowed. That righteous empowerment of both women and men—Saints—made possible the faithful accomplishment of many daunting tasks as they settled the American West and sought to establish their Zion.

What ideas motivated these women? From the original Relief Society, I have identified several core ideas, as important to us today as when the Relief Society was founded. First is an underlying faith in the Lord Jesus Christ. Faith in Christ, nurturing, and compassion are foundational. A fourth ideal is that of sisterhood, learning to "cherish one another."[10] The old *Relief Society Magazine* had a column called "Women's Sphere," which celebrated the accomplishments of women, most of them not Latter-day Saints. This tradition can be traced back to the *Woman's Exponent,* a periodical begun in 1870 for LDS women.[11] The masthead of the *Woman's Exponent* during much of its forty years read, "For the rights of the women of Zion and for the rights of the women of all nations." That is truly how these women saw themselves—in the vanguard, leading out in the righteous advancement of women.

These early women also saw themselves as bettering their communities and developing their own gifts and talents. Women first voted in Utah in February 1870. In granting the franchise to Utah women, the federal government was trying to embarrass LDS men. The social stigma against women in politics was enormous. Cartoons from the era depicted what would happen to a woman if she voted. She would *instantly* turn into an ugly, snarling, beefy feminist—right at the voting booth! They also thought that LDS women would vote out polygamy. Polygamy remained, and Utah women voted in great numbers.

In the same month that Utah women were freely voting for the first time, in Rochester, New York, suffragist Susan B. Anthony walked into a barbershop voting station and was refused a ballot. When they denied her the right to vote, she protested, citing the recently ratified Fourteenth and Fifteenth Amendments to the United States Constitution and pointing out that these amendments giving Negro men the franchise specify every "citizen" and "person" shall have a vote. Was she not a citizen? Was she not a person? In some confusion, they let her vote, but they also called a constable to arrest her. When the constable arrived, she insisted that she go in chains, as metaphor of the state of women.

Women in Utah continued to vote for seventeen years, from 1870 to 1887, until the Federal Edmunds Tucker Act disenfranchised the Church and denied voting rights for many LDS men as well as the women. After the Manifesto in 1890, the Relief Society devoted its efforts single-mindedly to getting the vote for women included in the proposed new state constitution. And they were ultimately successful, even over the opposition of such articulate opponents as B. H. Roberts.[12]

At this time, the national press rhetoric was still, "Oh, the poor oppressed women of Utah. They are under the thumbs of their husbands and their ecclesiastical leaders. They are the most oppressed of all women." Yet, running for one of five at-large state senate seats was Martha Hughes Cannon, a trained, practicing physician. Her husband was also running for an at-large state senate seat.[13] He was her stake president, which made him not only her husband but her ecclesiastical leader, too. She was running as a Democrat, and he as a Republican. She won. He lost. The national press scratched their heads. At that time very few women in the nation were allowed to vote, even fewer were running for office, and fewer still were winning—especially against their husbands. Susan B. Anthony, still without the vote in New York, had rightly said that her Latter-day Saint sisters were the freest women on the face of the earth. Relief Society sisters knew that freedom was their heritage, bestowed by the Prophet in Nauvoo. These early Utah women saw themselves empowered to act in righteous ways because they were women of covenant.

Around the turn of the century, Utah's bid for statehood and desire to become part of the United States influenced the character of Relief Society. At the time, the women's club movement was forging full steam ahead in American society. This model appealed to many Latter-day Saint women hoping to be less "peculiar." These clubs were of three kinds: the basic sewing circle, sometimes expanding to other arts and crafts; the social activist groups working for the betterment of society; and the cultural-literary club whose aims were usually self-education. The Relief Society became all of them! For the first time, Relief Society meetings were formally divided up with systematized lessons: religion one week; arts and crafts, sewing, and homemaking the next; social ideas the third week; and culture the fourth.

Now at the end of the twentieth century, what seems to be a new tack is actually harking back to how things were in the beginning. Our Relief Society leaders provide fewer directions, and we are left to figure out more for ourselves. I think of the worldwide sesquicentennial Relief Society projects in 1992. To figure things out for ourselves is sometimes a messy process, but we have been asked to continually be looking at our local group, discovering its changing needs, looking to see what we can do to better our communities, just as did our earliest Relief Society sisters in Nauvoo.

I welcome this return to the foundational ideas outlined in the original Relief Society minutes, the "something better" Joseph Smith prophesied. We are to be women with faith in the Lord Jesus Christ; we are to nurture, to be compassionate, to be sisters, to better our communities, and to develop our own gifts and talents. We are to do all of those things within the context of being women of covenant. We covenant first at baptism. We covenant again in the temple. And we renew those covenants weekly in partaking of the sacrament.

I see us in Relief Society reclaiming the heritage that has been ours, the "something better" which was not to be a sewing circle or women's club. To me that is the "So What?" of Relief Society. It opens vistas to me as a woman and prepares me for the temple, where I can lay foundations, receive inspiration, and commit my all to becoming all that my Heavenly Father desires for me.

NOTES

1. *A Centenary of Relief Society* [ed. Belle S. Spafford and Marianne C. Sharp] (Salt Lake City: General Board of Relief Society, 1942), 14.

2. Emma Smith, in *Centenary,* 14.

3. Sarah Cleveland, "A Record of the Organization, and Proceedings of the Female Relief Society of Nauvoo," 1842–1844, holograph, Archives of the Historical Department of The Church of Jesus Christ of Latter-day Saints, Salt Lake City, Utah, 17 Mar. 1842; hereafter cited as Nauvoo Minutes.

4. Nauvoo Minutes, 28 Apr. 1842; emphasis added.

5. George Albert Smith, "Address to the Members of the Relief Society," General Relief Society Conference, 4 Oct. 1945; in *Relief Society Magazine,* Dec. 1945, 717.

6. Reynolds Cahoon, Nauvoo Minutes, 13 Aug. 1843.

7. Seneca Falls is just at the other end of Seneca Lake from where the Church was organized at the Peter Whitmer farm eighteen years earlier.

8. Abigail Adams, *Adams Family Correspondence,* vol. 1, ed. L. H. Butterfield (Massachusetts Historical Society, 1963), 10–11.

9. John Adams, in *Correspondence,* 11.

10. See Lucy Mack Smith, Nauvoo Minutes, 24 Mar. 1842, 19.

11. In 1870 Brigham Young called his niece Louisa Lula Greene Richards, who was eighteen years old at the time, to be the editor of a new woman's publication. This was not an official Church publication—the idea of being "official" is a rather recent creation—but it was the voice of LDS women for more than forty years. Louisa had virtually no background that would have prepared her to do this, and she felt very inadequate. Nevertheless, she founded the journal. During her years as editor, she married, had a miscarriage, and became pregnant again. Because protecting this pregnancy was very important to her, she resigned her position as editor of the *Woman's Exponent.* The editorship then fell to Emmeline B. Wells, who was in her early forties at

the time. For almost forty years Emmeline continued as editor and only gave up the position when at age eighty-two she was called to be the general president of the Relief Society. (She felt she just could not do both jobs at the same time.) The *Woman's Exponent* was the first and longest lived women's publication west of the Mississippi.

12. B. H. Roberts was not in favor of women receiving the vote; not surprisingly, he was not a favorite among LDS women during this period. When Spencer W. Kimball was born, his father wanted to name him after B. H. Roberts. His mother strenuously objected, and so the future prophet was named Spencer Woolley instead. After the issue was decided, B. H. Roberts eventually made his peace with Mormon women. See Edward L. Kimball and Andrew E. Kimball Jr., *Spencer W. Kimball* (Salt Lake City: Bookcraft, 1977), 18–19.

13. On the ballot for the first election after statehood were all the state officers plus members of the state legislature and senate. State senators represented various districts, but five senators were also to be elected as representatives at-large.

PIETA

NANCY BAIRD

Lying on my mother's bed
listening to tropical rain skitter
across a mottled screen,
I hold my daughter, sprawled in sleep,
head pressed to my heart.
To the west
across a shifting silver sheet of water
the world falls endlessly away.
The child's leg twitches in a
white ginger dream,
my fingers round the curve of her
almond head.
According to some unspoken law of
hearts, the women in this house return love
only in the measure it is given
while you
continents, centuries away
hold your son like that,
your cheek gray and smooth as stone
your eyes cracked as crystals.
He slides from your knees
from the cradle of your grief.
Your right hand claims the broken body,

Nancy Hanks Baird received her bachelor's degree in English from Brigham Young University and is a freelance writer and editor. She and her husband, John K. Baird, are the parents of five children. She is the Gospel Doctrine teacher in her ward in Salt Lake City.

gathers him to your ribs,
your left hand gives him back,
offers with cupped grace
your two seamless souls
soundlessly, immutably
as marble.

WE MUST CHERISH ONE ANOTHER

AILEEN H. CLYDE

Scripture and our own Latter-day Saint history indicate a deeply rooted need in women—perhaps a female characteristic—to gather. Do you remember how quickly Mary of Nazareth went to her cousin Elisabeth for reassurance and support? Luke records that after the angel departed, "Mary arose . . . and went into the hill country with haste . . . and saluted Elisabeth" (Luke 1:39–40). Mary and Elisabeth, faced with momentous but deeply personal events that shook their lives and even their perceptions of themselves, turned to each other for confirmation, reassurance, and comfort. In each other, the cousins found empathy and strength as part of their blessing from the Holy Spirit.

I am convinced there are Elisabeths for every Mary. Such relationships are so worth having that women have long found ways to come together in combinations from two to twenty to hundreds, seeking light for their minds and nourishment for their feminine souls. In one another, we discover rich sources of spirituality, understanding, and comfort.

For LDS women, 1842 was a formative time. A society was created at women's initiative, with a prophet's authority, and with God's blessing. It was not a casual happening. Yet, many indicators suggest that today Relief Society is treated casually

Aileen H. Clyde has served as second counselor in the General Relief Society presidency. She and her husband, Hal M. Clyde, are the parents of three married sons. She has also served as vice chairman of the board of regents of the Utah System of Higher Education. She graduated from Brigham Young University and was an English instructor there.

by significant numbers of women for whom it was created. Could part of this passivity about our Society be the result of our not understanding or practicing the basic spiritual principles upon which it was founded?

Earlier this year, I received a phone call from a young female reporter assigned by a Utah newspaper to write an article about the founding of Relief Society. Besides where and when, she wanted to know by whom and why the Society was formed. As her questions proceeded, I found myself giving her more and more complicated responses. I referred her to the fine recent one-volume history of Relief Society, *Women of Covenant*. Then I asked if I could give her other LDS names as references to complete her assignment. She said, "Oh, I'm LDS and I go to Relief Society every week. I just don't know anything about its history."

Our Society's history matters; it is a way to begin understanding who we are and who we can be. Eliza R. Snow's minutes of the first two years' proceedings provide a rich report of our Society's beginnings. Her minutes show that at the second meeting on 24 March 1842, Counselor Elizabeth Ann Whitney spoke: "We must pray much for each other that we may succeed in the work before us and have wisdom given us in our pursuits."[1] Almost at the mention of the word *wisdom,* Mother Lucy Smith arose and addressed the group: "This institution is a good one—we must cherish one another, watch over one another, comfort one another and gain instruction that we may all sit down in heaven together."[2] Wisdom indeed! May I remind you that throughout the scriptures wisdom has been identified as a feminine quality? In the book of Proverbs, we read: "Doth not wisdom cry? and understanding put forth her voice? She standeth in the top of high places, by the way in the places of the paths. She crieth at the gates, at the entry of the city, at the coming in at the doors. . . . O ye simple, understand wisdom: and, ye fools, be ye of an understanding heart. . . . For wisdom is better than rubies; and all the things that may be desired are not to be compared to it" (Proverbs 8: 1–3, 5, 11).

Yes, Mother Smith, with all that we face today, just as did our sisters in 1842, we need wisdom. The wisdom you pronounced to us is that we can learn to cherish one another. You said that learning to cherish can have eternal, celestial consequences. What you said speaks to women's hearts today as it must have then—but now, as then, there are impediments. We struggle mightily to live the truths our souls confirm. We struggle for an understanding heart.

What does it mean to cherish one another? Let's turn again to our history. In *Women of Covenant,* this succinct distillation points us to an answer that suggests that cherishing is an inherently spiritual act: "At the fifth meeting of the Relief Society, on April 19, 1842, Counselor Sarah Cleveland expressed 'the happiness she felt in the present associations of females.' At that meeting sisters nurtured one another spiritually, exercising the gifts of the Spirit spoken of in the New Testament and the Doctrine and Covenants. Some bore testimony, others spoke in tongues and interpreted tongues, and, following the closing prayer and song, the sisters exercised the gift of healing on behalf of an ailing sister. The secretary commented that 'nearly all present arose & spoke, and the spirit of the Lord like a purifying stream, refreshed every heart.' Not only did these gifts remain with the women, but even more frequently, the sisters enjoyed the gifts spoken of in the New Testament as the 'word of wisdom' and the 'word of knowledge': that all-important gift to *know* by the power of the Holy Ghost that Jesus is the Christ."[3]

Those founding women experienced much that was spiritual. Such defining moments give us clarity and focus. That focus and faith in Christ makes Relief Society unique in the world. Reading Eliza's minutes, we see that "the society was not only to perform charitable work, but also to acquire and exercise the gift of charity, beginning within the group itself.

Emma Smith admonished her sisters to 'divest themselves of every jealousy and evil feeling toward each other.' And the prophet [who was with them] exhorted, 'Let your hearts expand. Let them be enlarged towards others—you must be long-suff'ring and bear with the faults and errors of mankind. How precious are the souls of men [and women]!—The female part of the community are apt to be contracted in their views. You must not be contracted, but you must be liberal in your feelings.'"[4]

Even with these great principles at work, our early sisters found perplexing problems. They wanted fervently to do good but were not always certain how to proceed. They were not sure, for instance, about whether and how to reach out to those they viewed as needing reform. In Christ's time there were sincere Pharisees quick to judge a deed and completely miss the principle. In our time, it may also be easier for us as women to judge than to cherish one another.

The Prophet Joseph Smith often visited those earliest Relief Society meetings. As the women sought to comprehend how best to exercise the gift of charity, they had the blessing of a prophet's immediate counsel. In June 1842 he said: "'Nothing is so much calculated to lead people to forsake sin as to take them by the hand and watch over them with tenderness.' He also noted that individuals who are 'unacquainted with the principle of godliness' display a 'contraction of feeling and lack of charity.' In contrast, 'the pow'r and glory of Godliness is spread out on a broad principle to throw out the mantle of charity. God does not look on sin with allowance, but when men [or women] hav sin'd there must be allowance made for them.'

"As far as the Prophet was concerned, . . . 'The Society is not only to relieve the poor but to save souls.' . . . Such is the end point of charity, 'the pure love of Christ.'"[5]

Mother Smith turned us towards that highest law when she admonished us to cherish. Cherishing implies holding dear, fostering, nurturing, promoting development or growth, and encouraging. The varied circumstances of women's lives today suggest that we too need ways to cherish that will inform our decisions and enlarge our capacities to act.

Did Lucy Smith have any idea LDS women would number more than 3.7 million throughout the world by 1995? Cherishing requires great expansion of our minds and hearts, accomplished only by guidance from the Holy Spirit, "for the Spirit speaketh the truth and lieth not. Wherefore, it speaketh of things as they really are . . . for the salvation of our souls" (Jacob 4:13).

Knowing how things really are is no small matter—if it involves the salvation of our souls. Remember Joseph Smith's counsel to "not be contracted, but . . . liberal in your feelings."[6] Did he mean we tend not to look beyond what is immediately before us in our daily routines? Let's broaden our view to women's circumstances worldwide. While making up half of the world's population, women today work two-thirds of the world's working hours. Their work yields them one-tenth of the world's wealth and one-hundredth of the world's land. Women form two-thirds of the world's illiterate people. More than three-fourths of starving people are women with their dependent children.[7]

In addition to those bleak facts, women and their female children are disproportionately vulnerable to exploitation, abuse, battering, rape, and murder. These general conditions for women in the world today reflect pain and injustice not acceptable to us or our God. These stark realities bring new meaning to our covenants. Surely women can be a powerful part of opening up more humane ways of living for all people. To effect such good depends on recognizing that we live by choices and can work toward becoming perfect by choosing well. This perfecting does not have flawless living as its aim; rather, perfecting is the exercise of agency amidst difficult choices that yields growth and progress.

Mother Eve is the first and best example of facing a great dilemma. Her soul-wrenching decision and its eternal consequences were right for her—and for us, too. I think of Eve as the prototype of human choice. I also revere her as the exemplar of the female power known as motherhood. Like choice, motherhood shares the inevitable companionship of both pain and joy. In its responsible manifestations, it represents ways of cherishing that are essential, both now and in eternity, to human development and growth. While it has a literal meaning of giving birth, motherhood also refers to the nascent capacity to love. Maternal-type love, while tender and compassionate, also has a toughness and tenacity that outlasts awful disappointment. Quick to sense anything that will thwart the development and growth of the young and the vulnerable, this love can suffer long and sacrifice. It parallels the love our Savior offers unconditionally by his grace. This love has nothing to do with deserving and everything to do with divine compassion meeting human need. Thus the maternal metaphor applies both to those who have given birth and also to those who may not have children but love in ways that nurture and renew or reform. We read in Isaiah: "As one whom his mother comforteth, so will I comfort you; and ye shall be comforted" (Isaiah 66:13). God, who knows his children's needs, compares maternal love with his power to give comfort. Perhaps that's our best evidence of woman's divine nature and potential. Such love has as its goal a homecoming, a returning to the source of our spiritual creation, a sitting down together in heaven.

Unfortunately, maternal love is often condescended to and trivialized by sentimental stereotypes such as those that plague Mother's Day celebrations. Often focused too narrowly on biological role designations, these events can chill a mother's heart with too much embarrassing praise. We might see maternal power more clearly in the mother bear. She nurtures and protects her cubs, and woe to the intruder who may pose a threat. Her fierceness demonstrates her commitment to caring as well as her maternal power to recognize and deflect danger. Most of what she does is instinctive, inbred, and quite uncomplicated. Her basic task is completed in a season; not so for us humans. Because of the long and crucial childhood of human children, maternal influence—we could call it "cherishing"—is essential to the physical, emotional, intellectual, and spiritual development of our young. We also know our need for such love persists throughout our lives.

As women we have several distinct characteristics. Beside motherhood, I'd place sisterhood as a paradigm of our particular strength. I don't know how long women had been "gathering" for support and mutual benefit, but in the book of Judges is an old and unexpected example, the story of Jephthah's daughter. Jephthah was described as the son of a harlot. Jephthah's father, Gilead, already had a wife and other sons, who in due time banished Jephthah, explaining, "For thou art the son of a strange woman," which was another way of saying she was a prostitute (Judges 11:2). In the first two verses of this story, Jephthah's mother is labeled with degrading names twice. Women, especially in their roles as mothers, have long been vulnerable to disparagement and harshness.

Jephthah grows up away from his people in the land of Tob. Known as "a mighty man of valour," he is strong and fierce enough that the Gileadites seek him out when they need a brave warrior to lead them in a crucial fight against the Ammonites. In spite of his "strange" mother, Jephthah was an Israelite. He reminded them of their earlier cruelty to him and exacted a promise that if he prevailed over their enemies, the Gileadites would make him their captain and leader. This was not a timid man. His next step was even more brash. "And Jephthah vowed a vow unto the Lord, and said, If thou shalt without fail deliver the children of Ammon into mine hands, Then it shall be, that whatsoever cometh forth of the doors of my house to meet me, when I return in peace from the children of Ammon, shall surely be the Lord's, and I will offer it up for a burnt offering" (Judges 11:30–31).

To be fair, this warrior had not had much nurturing; his religious instruction was obviously faulty. Anyone who knows God knows bargaining with him is not necessary. But the practice was, and is, widespread, and Jephthah made a foolhardy pledge. The record says he slew the children of Ammon in twenty cities "with a very great slaughter. Thus the children of Ammon were subdued before the children of Israel" (Judges 11:33).

Now Jephthah, fresh from victorious battle and evidently unharmed, returned home. Brave warrior, denied a mother's or a father's nurture, he only knew how to make war and keep brash bargains. I don't know what or whom he expected to see first on his return home, but these are the rich Hebraic images: "And Jephthah came to Mizpeh unto his house, and, behold, his daughter came out to meet him with timbrels and with dances: and she was his only child; beside her he had neither son nor daughter. And it came to pass, when he saw her, that he rent his clothes, and said, Alas, my daughter! thou has brought me very low, and thou art one of them that trouble me: for I have opened my mouth unto the Lord, and I cannot go back" (Judges 11:34–35).

All too human, he blames her for this awful mess. I have heard this story related as an example of a man keeping his word. Though that element is surely there, that's not why I'm telling it. The story matters most to me for the painful, joyful consequences I see portrayed as humans struggle to relate to God and one another. With the next turn, the story becomes an example not only of female courage but also of the cherishing sisterhood Lucy Smith pointed us toward.

"And she said unto him, My father, if thou hast opened thy mouth unto the Lord, do to me according to that which hath proceeded out of thy mouth. . . . Let this thing be done for me: let me alone two months, that I may go up and down upon the

179

mountains, and bewail my virginity, I and my [sisters]. And he said, Go. And he sent her away for two months: and she went with her companions, and bewailed her virginity upon the mountains.

"And it came to pass at the end of two months, that she returned unto her father, who did with her according to his vow which he had vowed: and she knew no man. And it was a custom in Israel, That the daughters of Israel went yearly to lament the daughter of Jephthah the Gileadite four days in a year" (Judges 11:36–40).

Does that remind you of a teaching in Mosiah about bearing one another's burdens and mourning with those who mourn and comforting those who stand in need of comfort? These Israelite women grew spiritually by remembering their love for Jephthah's daughter and her integrity four days a year. Can't we use that pattern for our meeting as sisters to help each other face life's difficulties, lest we all be overwhelmed by them?

In 1830, the Lord said to Emma Smith: "Verily I say unto thee that thou shalt lay aside the things of this world, and seek for the things of a better" (D&C 25:10). Our everyday life, however, demands our labor and commands our choices even as we yearn to ascend beyond our daily work. It's not easy to "lay aside . . . this world and seek for the things of a better." Other women's stories can help us find ways. My own grandmother gave me a treasured glimpse of her labor and her choices as she told me in quiet conversations of the challenges of her life. When she was in the sixth grade, a bright and able student, she had to leave school because as the oldest daughter she was needed at home. She eventually had twelve siblings and was her mother's constantly needed helper. Her formal education thus curtailed, one of the "things of a better" life she actively sought was learning. Gospel learning was her focus.

Grandmother married in 1888 and bore eleven children. Grandfather, described as idealistic, served as bishop for more than thirty years, while Grandmother managed their temporal necessities. Besides their own large family, at one time or another, she and her husband provided a home for seven other children. The intertwining of everyday life and gospel life, motherhood, and sisterhood are evident in this one day's entry in her journal:

"I arose quietly so as not to wake George or the others at 4:30 A.M. Too cold for kneeling prayer.

"Got the fire started and put bread in the pans. [The rule in the house was that the last one in at night mixed the bread for slow rising.] Got breakfast going before waking the girls. Helen took a half hour for her piano. Her playing makes the morning cheerful.

"We did 5 pies before they left for school. Making lunches was slow because the bread wasn't cool.

"I mopped the kitchen and ironed until time to get ready for Relief Society. [They met on Tuesday afternoon, and they all wore hats! Grandmother always walked the six blocks to church.] Had a very good theology lesson on our covenants. I love the scriptures and wish I had more time to understand them better.

"Decided to stop in at Sister Pryor's on my way home. Although much awaited me, I couldn't just walk by knowing she had been abed 6 weeks. Her bedroom curtains were nearly black. No one could feel better in such a room so I took them down and carried them home. [The pollution in Utah valley was frightful in those days when all heating and cooking was done with coal and wood. Spring and fall cleanings really were necessary.]

"We had 14 for supper again tonight. While things cooked, I washed and starched the curtains. We dried them on the stretchers behind the dining room stove. [Do you feel the understatement of her dinner preparations for fourteen in the phrase 'while things cooked'? Then add to that the task of curtain stretching. I recall the stretchers looked like quilt frames

181

stood on end with tiny pins all around the frame to hold the fabric borders taut.]

"I left for MIA early enough to get the curtains up. Sister Pryor was so relieved and grateful. It wasn't much for me but made a big difference to her.

"I was disappointed in the Mutual lesson. It wasn't worth the walk. Usually I'm glad I've made the effort.

"Tomorrow will be full of what I didn't get done today. I love the Lord. I don't know why I'm so weary."[8]

Can you hear that paradox? After listing an eighteen-hour working day of family tasks, church involvement, and sisterly service, she pens a record and wonders if she has accomplished anything—and then wonders at her weariness! I honor her steadfast progress through things of this world toward a very grand design.

In Alma 9:26 is a promise that brings comfort to any human heart seeking an antidote for the ills of this life: "And not many days hence the Son of God shall come in his glory; and his glory shall be the glory of the Only Begotten of the Father, full of grace, equity, and truth, full of patience, mercy, and long-suffering, quick to hear the cries of his people and to answer their prayers."

As we build on our rich tradition of cherishing one another, may we look together toward that day in full faith. When we gather, we find empathy and strength. When we labor together, we can accomplish much. It is our great honor to develop, as we go, those same qualities that will identify the Savior to us and us to him—grace, equity and truth, patience, mercy and long-suffering.

NOTES

1. Sarah Cleveland, "A Record of the Organization, and Proceedings of the Female Relief Society of Nauvoo," 1842–1844, holograph, Archives of the Historical Department of The Church of Jesus Christ of Latter-day Saints, Salt Lake City, Utah, 24 Mar. 1842, 18; hereafter cited as Nauvoo Minutes.

2. Ibid., 19.

3. Jill Mulvay Derr, Janath Russell Cannon, Maureen Ursenbach Beecher, *Women of Covenant: The Story of Relief Society* (Salt Lake City: Deseret Book, 1992), 36.

4. Ibid., 36.

5. Ibid., 37.

6. Ibid., 36.

7. "World's Women Data Sheet," *Report of the World Conference to Review and Appraise the Achievements of the United Nations Decade for Women: Equality Development and Peace* (New York: United Nations, 1985). Quoted in Alexander B. Morrison, "The Sobbings of Their Hearts," BYU Literacy Conference, 24 Mar. 1995, 3.

8. Sarah Ann Eliza Brockbank Hales, journal in possession of the author.

THE TURNING OF HEARTS IN THE BOOK OF MORMON

MARILYN ARNOLD

And he shall turn the heart of the fathers to the children, and the heart of the children to their fathers.
3 Nephi 25:6

One abiding theme of the Book of Mormon is that people who love the Lord also love each other. Another equally persistent theme is pride. Like love, it, too, is a matter of the heart because pride places worldly things—such as power, influence, wealth, and class—above considerations of innate human worth and need. Love is a softening of the heart; pride is a hardening.

On the subject of love, or lack of it, it is interesting to compare the two voyages to the new world that are described in the Book of Mormon. The first, undertaken by the Jaredites, is a model in cooperation and tranquillity. Jared and his brother are in accord, and any disagreements are worked through peaceably. The second, undertaken by Lehi's group, is the reverse, full of dissension and violence.

Apparently, scarcely a squabble ruffled the peace of the Jaredite group through the 344 days and nights at sea, for the

Marilyn Arnold is professor emeritus of English and former dean of graduate studies at Brigham Young University. A widely published writer and the recipient of several teaching and research awards and lectureships, she serves as Spiritual Living teacher in her ward Relief Society.

record says that day and night "they did sing praises unto the Lord" (Ether 6:9). Their arrival at the promised land was similarly sweet, for "they bowed themselves down upon the face of the land, . . . and did shed tears of joy before the Lord, because of the multitude of his tender mercies over them" (Ether 6:12).

A far cry from the optimistic tranquillity of the Jaredites is the experience of the Lehites. Their journey began on a tenuous note and was fraught with strife, animosity, disregard for others, and murderous intent. Instead of singing praises to God, Nephi's older brothers and some of Ishmael's children "began to make themselves merry, insomuch that they began to dance, and to sing, and to speak with much rudeness" (1 Nephi 18:9). Nephi's efforts to counsel them resulted in severe physical abuse, while Lehi's pleas fell on deaf ears. Lehi and Sariah nearly died of grief, and young Jacob and Joseph, along with Nephi's wife and children, shed many tears on that voyage. We are not surprised that upon arriving, Nephi merely says, "we went forth upon the land, and did pitch our tents; and we did call it the promised land" (1 Nephi 18:23). Despite the fertility of the promised land, the family rift that began in the wilderness outside Jerusalem eventually divided a nation and thwarted the hopes for a lasting covenant society.

The Jaredites had a happier beginning, but their promise, too, was shattered by the failure of human affection, particularly filial affection. The book of Ether presents only the sketchiest account of the succession of Jaredite kings, but it becomes apparent in generation after generation that the hearts of the children have turned from their fathers. King after king is slain by son after son, and countless brothers conspire against each other. Insurrectionists plot against monarchs and steal their thrones, friendships collapse, and God is forgotten by all but the prophets. In both the Lehite and the Jaredite nations, vast numbers of people forget their humanity, set aside their affections, and lose their very souls.

If this were the whole story of the Book of Mormon, it would be a grim book indeed. But it is not the whole story, not by any means. Some of the Book of Mormon's most powerful moments come when hearts are turned to God. And, invariably, that spiritual change produces an almost simultaneous turning to fellow beings. One of those precious instances of turning occurs during the reign of King Benjamin, as he addresses his people in a great outdoor gathering. Touched to the quick and brought to the depths of humility, they experience a great change of heart, and they receive a remission of their sins—the ultimate turning. But Benjamin clearly connects their being "filled with the love of God" and their "always retain[ing] a remission of [their] sins" (Mosiah 4:12) with a similar turning of their hearts to others, particularly to those in need. The outcome of this turning to Christ, he promises, is that they "will not have a mind to injure one another" but "will succor those that stand in need" and "administer of [their] substance unto" them (Mosiah 4:13, 16).

We are all familiar, too, with the younger Alma's eloquent sermon on the changing of hearts. He experienced a dramatic change himself, and he knew that his father had also experienced such a change. Like Benjamin, Alma links the turning of hearts toward God with a similar turning to fellow beings. Even as he describes the change of heart, he cautions against pride and envy, warning any who would "make a mock of his brother" or "heap . . . upon him persecutions" (Alma 5:30). These public expressions, Benjamin's and Alma's, are impressive and inspiring, but the Book of Mormon teaches the turning of human hearts by example as well as by sermon. Buried in its pages is one particularly touching account of reciprocal personal devotion.

We remember that Alma met stiff resistance when he attempted to teach the gospel in Ammonihah. The people there "withstood all his words, and reviled him, and spit upon him, and caused that he should be cast out of their city" (Alma 8:13).

Half-starved, Alma heads toward the city of Aaron. An angel intercepts him, but does the angel give him sympathy and relieve him of his duty? Not on your life. In fact, the angel's first words are hardly the words a man who has just been spit upon and reviled would expect or hope to hear. The angel says, "Blessed art thou, Alma; therefore, lift up thy head and rejoice, for thou hast great cause to rejoice" (Alma 8:15). Then the angel delivers a disheartening commission: Alma is told to return to Ammonihah. At first blush, the angel may seem a bit unfeeling, but he is most certainly looking out for Alma. The angel visits Amulek in Ammonihah and instructs him to care for a holy prophet who will ask him "for something to eat" (Alma 8:19–20), and Amulek does.

Alma "tarrie[s] many days with Amulek," so long, in fact, that the Lord has to nudge him to get on with his preaching (Alma 8:27–29). Amulek goes with him, willingly suffering whatever fate awaits his new friend. The bond of mutual belief has strengthened both men, spiritually and physically, and they set out "filled with the Holy Ghost" and endowed with heavenly power (Alma 8:30–31). Alma and Amulek together suffer imprisonment and torture, but of the two, Amulek makes the greater sacrifice for his faith. Whatever Alma endures in preaching the word, he still has friends and family and home to return to. Not so Amulek. He has "forsaken all his gold, and silver, and his precious things, which were in the land of Ammonihah, for the word of God, he being rejected by those who were once his friends and also by his father and his kindred" (Alma 15:16). Amulek has given up everything that he had valued before Alma came—home and wealth, yes, but more devastating still, family and friends.

It is appropriate that the narrative comes full circle. Alma takes a spent and broken-hearted Amulek home with him to Zarahemla, "to his own house," where he "did administer to him in his tribulations, and strengthened him in the Lord"

(Alma 15:18). Alma returns the care and devotion that Amulek had once rendered him.

The Book of Mormon also contains striking instances of individual sympathy of another kind: examples of caring that do not necessarily involve physical acts of charity or service. There are persons who demonstrate an unusual capacity for empathy, for extraordinary feeling. One of those is Jacob, Nephi's younger brother. Although we cannot readily detect it in Jacob's highly sophisticated sermon in 2 Nephi, Jacob is very tender-hearted. He is also conscientious in the extreme. That he is not chosen to rule after Nephi suggests, too, that his gifts are spiritual rather than political.

Responding to divine direction, Jacob undertakes to instruct the Church on the men's hardness of heart, pride, and marital infidelity. The assignment is anything but easy for Jacob; he hates confronting the husbands with their shameful behavior. More than that, however, he loathes inflicting still more pain on their already suffering wives and children. He is aggrieved, he says, that he "must use so much boldness of speech . . . before [their] wives and [their] children, many of whose feelings are exceedingly tender and chaste and delicate" (Jacob 2:7). Jacob's sensitivity to the feelings of the women and children in his congregation and his desire to lift them rather than to increase their pain are apparent throughout his sermon. I do not recall seeing that extreme sensitivity, that deeply affecting concern for the emotional vulnerability of others, demonstrated more poignantly anywhere else in scripture—nor have I seen anything quite like it in a lifetime of church meetings.

We seldom pause to consider the nature of the man from whom such words come, and yet we can learn as much from his example in human sympathy as from his doctrinal teachings. How often do we measure, in advance, the consequences in injured feelings of our words, especially those we deliver in the presence of the innocent? We sometimes assume that justified righteous indignation relieves us of the obligation of sympathy. Jacob teaches us that it does not.

Others in the Book of Mormon also teach us important lessons in human sympathy. The book portrays several fathers whose hearts are turned to their sons. For example, we see great feeling in the patriarchal blessings Lehi pronounces on his sons, even the wicked ones, and in the blessings Alma and Helaman pronounce on their sons. In particular, Alma's words to the careless Corianton, words full of anguish and worry, show his great love for this inconstant son. Not only does Alma repeatedly use the term "my son," but he takes time to answer Corianton's doctrinal questions fully, thus showing his respect for the young man's mind and his potential for change. Alma's own willful youth perhaps created a special sympathy for the feelings and weaknesses of others.

Especially touching are the two letters from Mormon to his son Moroni, both written in the thick of battle (Moroni 8 and 9). The first is largely matter-of-fact and administrative, setting forth the doctrine forbidding infant baptism. Nevertheless, before Mormon addresses the doctrinal matter, which is of great concern to him, he first expresses his deep love for his son and his joy in Moroni's calling. "My beloved son, Moroni," he opens, "I rejoice exceedingly that your Lord Jesus Christ hath . . . called you to his ministry, and to his holy work. I am mindful of you always in my prayers" (Moroni 8:2–3). We sense a deep mutual affection between father and son, an affection that stands in stark contrast to some of the Jaredite father-son relationships chronicled in the book of Ether.

Mormon's second letter is more personal, detailing the grief and barbarity that marked the closing days of the Nephite nations. But that letter is also punctuated with tenderness, for Mormon frequently addresses Moroni as "my beloved son." And near the end of his letter, he verbalizes a prayer of great solicitude for his son's feelings: "My son, . . . may not the things which I have written grieve thee, to weigh thee down unto death; but may Christ lift thee up, . . . and the hope of his glory and of eternal life, rest in your mind forever" (Moroni 9:25). Here, indeed, is a father whose heart is turned toward his child. And Moroni's regard for his father leads him to engrave these two splendid discourses into the record for the ages.

Nephi is another son whose heart is turned toward his father. In fact, one thing that distinguishes Nephi from his older brothers Laman and Lemuel is the honor he accords his father. Where they are critical of their father and obviously consider him a doddering visionary, Nephi never fails to show respect for Lehi, his prophetic calling, and his position as family patriarch. So long as Lehi is alive, Nephi defers to him, obeying his injunctions, reporting to him on completion of assignments, and in all things supporting and venerating him.

Perhaps the most striking example of a child's heart that is turned to a parent is Jesus himself. The abbreviated record of his ministry among the Nephites, reported in 3 Nephi, is replete with references to the Father. And always, always, Jesus makes a point of telling his listeners that he obeys his Father in all things.

On the subject of the changing or turning of hearts in the Book of Mormon, we could expound almost endlessly—the people of the elder Alma who established a society without blemish at the waters of Mormon; King Lamoni and his queen; Lamoni's father, who was willing to sacrifice both his kingdom and his sins to learn of Christ; the people of Ammon, converted Lamanites who chose to die rather than to kill, even in their own defense; the penitent people whom Jesus taught with such power that two centuries of peace ensued. And with all these groups, like the people in King Benjamin's vast congregation, the turning of hearts to Christ meant the turning of hearts to one another. The Savior also linked the two when he defined the great commandments as love of God and love of neighbor.

If we think we can love God and disregard the feelings of

our fellow beings, we are sadly mistaken. If the earth is visited with a curse, a possibility Malachi foresaw, it will surely be, as Malachi also foresaw, because the hearts of mortal children and mortal parents—the hearts of all of us—are turned *from* rather than *toward* the Lord and therefore from rather than toward each other (see Malachi 4:6).

MEDIA IMAGES OF WOMEN

CHERYL B. PRESTON, SHARON L. SWENSON, SUZANNE BARNES ENGEMANN

Cheryl: In the early 1960s, United States prosecutors charged the producers of a French film with marketing obscene material. The producers appealed all the way to the Supreme Court. The Supreme Court's opinion carved an obscure, complex, and virtually incomprehensible definition of *obscene* and then decided that this film did not qualify. In a concurring opinion, Justice Potter Stewart rebuked the court for its cumbersome attempt to define obscenity, concluding with these immortal words: "I shall not today attempt further to define the kinds of material I understand to be [obscene] and perhaps I could never succeed in intelligibly doing so. But *I know it when I see it,* and the motion picture involved in this case is not that" [emphasis added].[1]

Unless we are involved in government regulation or community activism, Latter-day Saints rarely deal with hard-core

Cheryl B. Preston, professor of law at the J. Reuben Clark Law School, Brigham Young University, teaches banking and finance and women's issues in law. She and her husband, Stanley J. Preston, are the parents of three children. Cheryl serves as a Gospel Doctrine teacher in her Bountiful, Utah, ward.

Sharon Lee Esplin Swenson, assistant professor of theater and film at Brigham Young University, specializes in critical studies in film history and theory and is interested in gender and family in film. Sharon and her husband, Paul Swenson, are the parents of two children. She teaches the Gospel Doctrine class in her Salt Lake City, Utah, ward.

Suzanne Barnes Engemann, an actress and model, has worked in New York and Los Angeles for many years. She and her husband, Paul R. Engemann, are the parents of one son. Suzanne is the Young Women Mia Maid activities counselor in her Provo, Utah, ward.

pornography. Even without firsthand experience, most of us know what constitutes hard-core pornography and why it is destructive—*we know it without seeing it.*

What we sometimes overlook are the more subtle moral and spiritual implications of commonplace images in our homes and offices. We fail to recognize the potentially dangerous messages contained in magazine and television advertisements. Moreover, we may actually encourage and perpetuate such images by purchasing the products these images sell. In short, *we don't know it when we see it.*

WHAT IS IT?

The line between pornography and merely tasteless material is imprecise. Hard-core fades into soft-core at some point, and soft-core fades into indirect or camouflaged pornography. Because camouflaged pornography is pervasive and subtle, it is uniquely dangerous.

Efforts to control hard-core pornography, although important, should not ignore the dangers of camouflaged pornography. Law professor Nadine Strossen warns, "Given the pervasive presence of sexist, violent imagery in mainstream American culture, most such imagery would remain intact, even if 'pornography' could be effectively suppressed. Moreover, because the mainstream imagery is viewed by far more people than is 'pornography,' and because it has the stamp of legitimacy, it has a greater impact on people's attitudes."[2]

Jean Kilbourne, who has been studying for more than twenty years how women are portrayed in advertising, suggests that, though people do not typically admit they are influenced by media images, "Americans are very culturally conditioned by ads, and children are particularly vulnerable to them."[3]

Advertisements condition us to accept as normal, and even to prefer, the images they present. One advertiser experimented with a commercial featuring a "real" woman—average size, features, and abilities. Women in the test audience hated

193

the commercial and were, in fact, brutal in expressing their dislike of the "real" woman in the ad.[4] Should that alarm us? If media images of physical beauty lead us to demean other qualities in ourselves, then yes, we should be concerned. Claudia Bepko and Jo-Ann Krestan agree: "For many women, self-image becomes almost totally identified with body image. If they look good, they are good. But if, in their own estimation, they don't measure up, they may experience some serious and painful feelings of self-loathing."[5]

Because we have been socialized to regard our normal selves as inadequate, we prefer seeing women in ads who are either inhumanly perfect or not whole women at all—just bodies or parts of bodies. Body parts and body-only shots are a staple of camouflaged pornography.

For instance, advertisers use women's bodies to sell everything from cars to men's shoes. Why show a Karastan oriental rug on an ordinary floor when we can drape it around a naked woman? Buffalo Blue Jeans backpacks seem more interesting when the entire backside of the model is arrayed in nothing but the pack. If voluptuous chests are the only way to sell products, I prefer the milk campaign featuring Naomi Campbell. Although the predominant feature in the picture is her breasts, which are too large to quite fit in her "super-tight, little black dress," at least milk is arguably a "related" product.[6]

As if to emphasize that it is the *body,* not the woman, that is important, ads often show only parts of bodies—typically not faces or eyes, but interchangeable parts, without individuality. As you flip through magazines, notice how many ads show women looking down, with closed eyes, or simply pictured from the neck down. One blatant example is a Gianni Versace ad for a beaded vest. The vest is open, exposing most of the model's breasts; her eyes are completely blindfolded with a matching scarf.

Even when the body parts depicted are not overtly sexual, this fragmentation is dangerous. Fragmented ads objectify

194

women as things, rather than people; human beings become commodities. A faceless chest or thigh is not perceived as part of a person. Depersonalized objects are easier for soldiers to kill or for rapists to rape. Soldiers are trained to regard their enemies as not fully human. Rapists also depersonalize their victims. In interviews, convicted rapists frequently speak of their victims as "it," not "her."[7]

Some ads do more than just objectify women as sexual objects; they actually perpetuate specific rape myths. Notorious for their rape themes are the recent Calvin Klein ad campaigns. One ad for Calvin Klein's Obsession cologne for men shows a naked woman, slung over a naked man's shoulder, being passively carried off. This ad depicts a pose uncommon in a healthy modern dating relationship, but not uncommon in the dynamics of rape. A similar ad for Guess jeans features a man carrying a kicking, screaming woman. On the next page, she sits in the back seat of a car looking ravaged.[8]

These ads consciously and unconsciously link violence to sexual gratification.[9] They suggest that women like to be carried off and overpowered physically and that doing so is both acceptable and "manly."

Another rape myth perpetuated by media images is that women actually mean yes when they say no. An ad for Macy's department store and Lagerfeld Photo Fragrance for Men shows a series of film frames in which a photographer forces his way into a model's dressing room as she clutches a towel for covering. By the last frame her attitude seems to have changed from aversion to enjoyment.

Rape and violence against women have become a national epidemic. Advertisements sometimes perpetuate an unhealthy link between sex and violence.

IS PORNOGRAPHY THE ONLY PROBLEM?

Sharon: The hidden messages Cheryl has been discussing are conveyed even more insidiously in film. In TV advertising,

195

movement and music plant images inside our psyche, and repeated viewings reinforce them. If our guard is down, they can pit us against each other and, worse, against ourselves. Far from being knit together in love, we may unravel in discouragement over never feeling quite good enough—not unless we wear size five designer jeans, tone up our skin color, polish our nails and teeth, spiral wave our hair, wash, brush, gloss, deodorize, perfume, accessorize, and then refresh our flagging spirits with a name-brand soft drink. The ever-changing criteria of what constitutes the ideal woman are impossible for any one individual to satisfy—without airbrushing, makeup and hair crews, computerized enhancements, and photographic touchup.

I am guilty. I am a co-conspirator. In my own home are two parents, one seventeen-year-old daughter, one thirteen-year-old son, two cats, one dog, one chameleon, two fish, and two polliwogs. In our bathtub/shower we have five kinds of shampoo, four conditioners, and four razors: two pink disposables, my Trac II, and our son's Trac II. (He doesn't shave just yet, but he's prepared.) My husband's electric razor is downstairs. We have two shaving soaps—a manly foam and a womanly gel—and three kinds of soap—two deodorant bars and one scented liquid. Plus we have antibacterial soap at the sink. Do we really need all these products?

One popular commercial, the Diet Coke midmorning office break, features strip-tease music and a reversal-of-gender stereotype: a group of office women share a bonding moment at the window ogling a construction worker. The singer croons: "I don't want you to be no slave, I don't want you to work all day, but I want you to be true. . . . And I just want to make love to you, love to you, uh hummm, yuh." The admiring women say, "See you tomorrow" to each other and shown in print is the phrase: "This is refreshment." We laugh and excuse the lie.

In one way or another, without malice, most commercials

lie to us. They tell us that if we use a certain product, we will be captivating. Another product will make us glamorous and beautiful. The Diet Coke ad tells us (among other things) that Diet Coke will make us sexually desirable. The hidden message in commercials, the dangerous lie, is that love is conditional—I will be loved only if I look right, smell right, buy right.

A need to feel loved, attractive, competent, or happy is a real need. But advertising strategies also create new, unthought-of "needs." Some ads make us want their product by telling us that we must have certain qualities and that their product is the only way to get those qualities.

Even though we are daughters of God, with eternal spirits, laboring on this earth to develop our unique qualities, these ads tell us that without their products and complete physical beauty, we are not good enough and cannot be happy. Our hair is not good enough, our smell is not good enough, our bodies are not good enough. *We are not good enough as we are.* All these ads have a common message: our absolute insufficiency to exist without their products.

The world of television commercials is a world of surfaces and first impressions. In this world, we are judged not by what we do, think, or are but by *how we look.* We must even use products to achieve a "natural look." If we need products to achieve the "natural look," imagine what we need to look glamorous! We *need* all these products simply to be passable.

Sometimes advertisers use the guise of entitlement or self-fulfillment as the justification for purchasing their product. A glamorous model in a mink tells us, "I'm worth it." But the ad still reinforces the secondary message that we are not good enough as we are. Advertisers also may suggest, perhaps unintentionally, that we cannot be happy without certain qualities, such as youth, which no product can give us.

Note that all ads are for consumable material things that are irrelevant to our permanent, deeper needs. The scriptures warn us not to spend our money for "that which is of no worth, nor

[to] labor for that which cannot satisfy" (2 Nephi 9:51). But in the torrent of modern media images, a woman is fighting the tide in her efforts to "hunger and thirst after righteousness" (3 Nephi 12:6). We must consciously resist wasting our lives "needing" more and more products.

Even though we are exposed to images of women in a variety of media, including television shows and news as well as commercial films, print ads, and television, commercials are the most effective way to change how we think about women's roles. They contain the most concise messages and are subject to the least examination. They are persuasive because they are multilayered, combining visual, verbal, and narrative elements. Also, we fail to scrutinize them because they catch us with our guards down: ads happen so quickly and are so common that they are just background noise in most homes. We dismiss them as silly, nonsensical, or irritating—but they have a great deal to do with the unacknowledged assumptions operating both politically and socially in our world.

Consider, for instance, our assumptions about men and women. Despite the fact that most commercials are addressed to women, commercials assume a stereotyped male point of view.[10] This perspective is not a loving, Christlike male point of view but an artificially critical perspective that reduces both men and women to stereotypes. It implies that men value women because of certain limited characteristics that can be perceived quickly; beauty tops the list.

To some extent, ads also suggest that women's work is not really important. How do you keep your house spotless? You buy a product and twenty seconds later the whole house is transformed. There is new wallpaper, new linoleum on the floor, and the housewife just had a manicure. Women in the home are frequently portrayed as perpetually bouncy, bright, and bubbly. Whatever they are doing, it is not any more serious than deciding what color hair to have, what toilet bowl freshener to buy, or what to microwave for supper. There is no real work involved in what women do.

This attitude about women's work makes women *objects* and men *actors*. Over and over again, ads depict women preparing themselves to be looked at and admired by men—and by other women, who judge them. The men in ads make the decisions, control what happens, solve mysteries, and resolve problems. In 95 percent of television ads, for instance, male voices show up with the products that solve the problem posed in the ad.[11] Women are primarily concerned with looking beautiful and with maintaining beautiful homes. "Women are sex objects, and men are success objects," points out Jean Kilbourne. "The emphasis for men is money and power and the goods that go with that, while for women it's youth and beauty and thinness."[12] Thus, commercials flatten both men and women, making them one-dimensional. Both sexes are cheated of their full complexity and vulnerability as human beings.

HOW DOES THE ADVERTISING INDUSTRY WORK?

Suzanne: We all experience the gap between reality on and off screen in different ways. My name may not be familiar to you, but I have been directly involved for twenty years as an actress and model in selling you many things. Advertising has been a rewarding career for me.

Because messages in ads may distract us from pursuing what is truly important, we have focused exclusively on harmful messages. Let me put advertising messages in another perspective. Ads are completely focused on the outward person; they are not meant to give you internal or eternal validation. They are meant to sell you a product. Advertisers use society's values to appeal to viewers. Certainly the media does affect our attitudes, but the cause-effect sequence is not always easy to sort out. Which came first, the chicken or the egg? Our interest in visual beauty is part of our eternal nature, not a vice. Something innate in us prefers beauty over the banal. The

199

motive behind the Karastan oriental carpet ad, for instance, may well be an appeal to this trait in us rather than a more prurient one.

Our concern is not to suggest you quit caring about how you look, smell, or dress (ditto for your house) but to encourage you to resist an emphasis on appearances to the exclusion of spiritual values. Only our connection with God can make us feel "good enough."

Now let me tell you a bit about how the advertising industry works. The bottom line in advertising is money. Advertising "generates $130 billion annual[ly], diet industry revenues have been put at $33 billion, 'youth' cosmetics at $20 billion, and cosmetic surgery at $300 million."[13] Because of the money involved, advertisers take care to use what works.

The details in commercials that seem incidental and casual are neither. A great deal of money is spent every year test marketing to find out what we, the public, will buy and how best to sell it to us. Decisions regarding the setting, lighting, music, wardrobe, makeup, hair, dialogue, and action are carefully made in board rooms with access to pages of demographics. The shape and coloring of a product also become an issue. My hair has been dyed for a commercial because it competed with the color of the bottle of shampoo being advertised.

Because of limited time and space, the advertising industry depends on shorthand messages to shape our perceptions. Advertisers use this method to encourage us to form an opinion or judgment quickly. The idea that brighter colors in your laundry means happiness is more easily shown by a smiling mom than said. Shorthand messages can be useful, but we need to be aware of them. They tend to be highly manipulative, promote stereotypes, and encourage us to accept an artificial ideal of perfection that is unhealthy and, ultimately, unattainable. They promise us status, success, acceptance, and popularity, if we use the right products.

Advertisers also use other techniques to evoke certain

emotional responses. For instance, advertisements press our insecurity buttons: "Raise your hand if you're SURE." They can make us feel guilty: "All 'good' mommies buy JIF." Ads play on our need for love and romance: "I can't seem to forget her. Her Windsong stays on my mind."

Advertisers and the media in general sometimes grab our attention by annoying or shocking us. The whole idea of advertising is to plant a message we remember; sometimes a negative message is as effective as a positive message in selling a product. We can often name the products whose ads irritate us most. Controversy also leads to free publicity and, negative or not, generates awareness of a product. That also means that ads using camouflaged and soft pornography are increasing because a product benefits from any kind of publicity, even public outcry.

Not all ad campaigns are sexual, demeaning, or inherently misleading. Advertising does provide a valuable service to the consumer. But as consumers, we need to be aware of advertisers' techniques so that we can maintain a healthy perspective and make educated choices. We are responsible for filtering out harmful messages which can affect our emotional, economic, and spiritual lives.

The world of television commercials is, of necessity, a world of first impressions. Everyday life is not much different. What is the first thought that pops into your head when you see someone in a ripped T-shirt and dirty jeans? What about someone in a designer suit and expensive shoes? Did advertising force you to these thoughts? Letting the material world distract us from what really matters is a problem but "hungering and thirsting after righteousness" need not exclude a nice appearance.

I was once told by an LDS director that he could not give me a part in a Church film because, as he put it, "No one would ever believe you as a Mormon mother; you're too pretty, too sophisticated looking"! I don't expect to get every job I audition for, but I was hurt by the director's comment. I *am* a Mormon mother. What does a "Mormon mother" look like, anyway? I would venture to say that she might look very different in the Amazon rainforests of Peru than she would in a sacrament meeting in Utah. The experience taught me that even within our own church culture, some people have a narrow idea of what a "true Mormon" should look like, even though this "ideal" has nothing to do with the gospel. Judging by looks alone means misjudging. This kind of misjudgment promotes competition and discouragement and pits women against other women.

As sisters in the gospel, we need to support and encourage each other's individuality in all ways. We need to allow each other to be who we are by seeing each other as daughters of God instead of judging who looks most like any particular culture's vision of ideal.

Cheryl: Ads are a problem only if they confuse or distract us from pursuing what is truly important. If we recognize their influence, we can counteract harmful messages.

To loosely paraphrase Justice Stewart, we have not attempted to define precisely the kinds of material that are always harmful. In fact, we each have our own opinions about that. But we seek to raise awareness. As we become more conscious of the subtle influence of ideas, we can make decisions in our homes about what is harmful. Once we learn to *know it when we see it,* we can take steps to resist demeaning and damaging messages.

Consider one last scripture—with a few additions to liken it unto ourselves. I hope in this new context it will suggest a meaning of loving ourselves without worrying about our surface beauty. God made us beautiful—as we are, and in all our varieties. Jesus speaks of the wild lilies of the field, not hothouse roses, when he says: "And why take ye thought for raiment? Consider the lilies of the field, how they grow; they toil not, neither do they spin [and they diet not, neither do they color their hair]: and yet I say unto you, That even [Cindy Crawford] in all [her] glory was not arrayed like one of these" (Matthew 6:28–29; see also D&C 84:82).

NOTES

Cheryl gratefully acknowledges the assistance of Sherrine M. Walker, Lisa Stamps-Jones, and Mary Thompson.

1. *Jacobellis v. Ohio,* 378 U.S. 184, 197 (1967) (Stewart, J., concurring).

2. Nadine Strossen, "A Feminist Critique of 'The' Feminist Critique of Pornography," *Virginia Law Review* 79 (1993): 1186.

3. Jean Kilbourne, in "Advertisers Still Lagging behind the Times," by Nina Burleigh, *Chicago Tribune,* 7 Apr. 1991, C8.

4. Jeffry Scott, "Selling with Sexism: Resurgence of Hot Ads Fuels Social, Political Battle over Unequal Treatment," *Atlanta Journal and Constitution,* 24 Nov. 1991, H1.

5. Claudia Bepko and Jo-Ann Krestan, *Too Good for Her Own Good* (New York: HarperPerennial, 1990), 15.

6. The ad copy reads in part: "Milk, it's just what my body needs. Well, that and a closet full of ultrashort, supertight, little black dresses."

7. Teresa Hommel, "Images of Women in Pornography and Media," *New York University Review of Law & Social Change* 8 (1978–79): 211.

8. Scott, "Selling with Sexism," H1.

9. Marianne Wesson, "Girls Should Bring Lawsuits Everywhere . . . Nothing Will Be Corrupted: Pornography as Speech and Product," *University of Chicago Law Review* 60 (1993): 851.

10. Naomi Wolf, *The Beauty Myth: How Images of Beauty Are Used Against Women* (New York: AnchorDoubleday, 1991), 165.

11. Hilary DeVries, "The New Women in the Eyes of the Media," *Christian Science Monitor,* 21 June 1984, 24.

12. Jean Kilbourne, quoted in Burleigh, *Chicago Tribune,* C8.

13. Carlin Meyer, "Sex, Sin, and Women's Liberation: Against Porn-Suppression," *Texas Law Review* 72 (1994): 1174.

"NEITHER SHALT THOU BURY THY TALENT"

BONNIE L. GOODLIFFE

There may be women who can be super wives and mothers, work full time, sew all the family's clothes, bake their own bread from home-grown wheat, and (as I heard Erma Bombeck say once) wash and iron their scraps of aluminum foil, but I am not one of them. The things I do, I try to do well. But I can't do everything and have stopped trying. What is more, now that I am past fifty, I have stopped apologizing for what I don't do. I have discovered this basic truth: when we're twenty, we are terribly concerned with what others think about us; at thirty-five, we become less concerned with what others are thinking about us; when we're fifty, we realize that hardly anyone *is* thinking about us.

I am not very domestic. My motto has been, "In twenty years, my house will not remember me." Therefore, I refuse to give it my best time. Instead, as a professional organist—performer and teacher—I spend a lot of time practicing. I average two to three hours a day in practice plus more time for rehearsal and performance. People occasionally express surprise when they hear me practicing. They don't realize that even a frequent performer still needs to practice scales and

Bonnie Lauper Goodliffe serves as Temple Square Organist and also teaches Relief Society in her ward. She and her husband, Glade P. Goodliffe, are the parents of seven children. She is a Fellow in the American Guild of Organists.

other technical exercises. Some are surprised that I need to practice at all. Yet I practice more now than I ever did as a student. I practice more now because I am expected to perform at a professional level, and every minute of practice pays off eventually.

Even more important to me than my music is my family. Only the two youngest are still at home full time. The others all live out of state. One is a junior in college, one is a missionary in South America, and three are in graduate school. None is married yet. I have invested a great deal of my time and energy in my children, doing the standard parenting things such as driving car pools, being soccer team mother, and sewing costumes for dance recitals. My children are some of my best friends. They don't need much car pooling now, but they sometimes flatter me by asking my advice.

I have deliberately promoted my children's independence—for their welfare as well as my own. I have tried to emulate my own mother whose philosophy was, "Be sure that you are still somebody after your children are gone. Do not make your identity synonymous with your children. You should have some independent purpose and existence, not just be an extension of other people, even good people." I believe we do our children no favor by waiting on them. Service is a fine principle, but children should not think of their parents as servants.

I am also a strong believer in exercise, and I wish that I had been converted to it earlier in my life. Physical exercise enables me to think more productively. A guiding principle I have followed is, When the mind is tired, exercise the body; when the body is tired, exercise the mind. In the past I have participated in aerobic exercise classes. Currently I walk about thirty minutes a day, usually alone. It is my meditation time. And I believe that music is a form of mental exercise.[1]

These are some of the life choices I have made. These choices, the things that are important to me and the way I invest my time, have defined who I am and what I now can do. I have a very powerful sense of stewardship. I feel strongly that, for reasons unknown to me, I have been granted certain abilities and opportunities but that I will be held accountable for what I do with them. I am under obligation to use these gifts in the Lord's service. That has not been a burden to me; it has been a great blessing. But some of the lessons I have learned have been unexpected.

I have been playing at the Salt Lake Tabernacle since 1979. My principal assignments are to accompany the Mormon Youth Chorus and Symphony in their rehearsals and performances and to play Tabernacle organ recitals for tourists. I also play for regional conferences, firesides, and other special meetings. I occasionally accompany the Mormon Tabernacle Choir in the "Music and the Spoken Word" broadcast. Even after fifteen years, I am still surprised to be playing at the Tabernacle. I had never aspired to the job. In fact, the job I have now didn't exist when I was an organ student. Playing the organ wasn't even my idea—it was my mother's way to keep me busy when my college piano teacher went on a sabbatical. Being an organist was all quite accidental.

I studied organ for six years in college, three of those years as a graduate student. I gave my graduate solo recital when I was six months pregnant with my first child. My husband Glade and I earned master's degrees at the same time; then he went to work, and I stayed home as I had always planned. If I wanted to practice the organ, I had to go to the church. For the three years we lived in Cleveland, Ohio, church was almost thirty miles away, and my practicing suffered.

When we were transferred to California and sold our house in Cleveland, we made enough money that my husband thought we should use it to buy an organ. It was a very sub-stantial investment, but the profit on the sale of the house was almost enough for an organ. I borrowed the rest of the money from my parents and paid it back from my piano teaching.

Buying the organ was a turning point in my life. I started to practice again. Within a year, we had been transferred again, quite unexpectedly, to Salt Lake City, where my life was to change dramatically.

In the summer of 1979, I was in the Primary presidency in my ward. Primary was then held on a weekday. One afternoon, as my children and I returned home from Primary, we heard the phone ringing. It was Robert Cundick, then senior organist at the Tabernacle. He asked if I would be interested in auditioning for a six-month guest organist calling at the Tabernacle. I still don't know how he got my name. I have thought quite a bit lately about my response to his question. Because I had just walked in the door, because it was so unexpected, I gave a very uncharacteristic response: I said yes. Normally I would have given a long, detailed list of why this was not a good time, not a reasonable request, and why I was not perfectly qualified for the position. Listing reasons why something cannot possibly work is one of my specialities. But on that one, rare occasion, I said yes. And it has altered the course of my life.

Let me tell you a few other things about myself that I don't usually talk about. I hope that I appear confident, well-prepared, disciplined, and in control. That is my public persona. I don't know how I could possibly perform without these qualities. They are not, however, the real me. I am in reality quite shy, very sensitive to criticism, and anxious to have others like me and approve of what I do. My real self sits in the car and cries after doing poorly on an organ exam or after making conspicuous errors in a performance. My real self is very fragile. But I frequently call upon my public persona to get me through tough situations. It can be very useful, but it is not really me.

Performers must do many things right simultaneously, stay very focused, and, above all, play accurately. As a performer, I must be able to recover quickly when something goes wrong (and you may be assured that something will go wrong). And I must be able to get through all of this without any distress registering on my face, because I may be on camera at any time. Of course, that is just acting.

In my music life, I can make and rely on certain assumptions. I have had enough training and experience as a performer to know that with sufficient practice and preparation time, I can perform almost entirely without errors. I very seldom get that kind of practice and preparation, but I believe an error-free performance is possible under ideal circumstances. I know what it requires: concentration, discipline, hard work, and time.

I know that careful preparation pays off. If I work through every conceivable problem mentally before I perform, I can overcome or eliminate most problems. I can even overcome a certain amount of performance anxiety ahead of time. I typically experience my worst anxiety in the days just before a major performance. I am usually quite composed for the performance itself.

Real life, however, is not like that. No amount of discipline on my part, no amount of planning or concentration, no amount of intelligence or study, no amount of time or hard work can assure me a life free of mistakes. I would prefer it to be otherwise. That has been a hard lesson for me to learn. My discipline, hard work, and choices are not the only deciding factors in my life. I am affected, positively and negatively, by everyone and everything around me. An infinite number of variables are at work which are impossible to control.

The very nature of mortals is that we make mistakes and that we will be affected by the mistakes of others. That is why we need the Savior. That is why we need the Atonement. What small part of this concept I now understand, I have learned from contrasting real life with my music life, where some of the laws are just the opposite.

One of the reasons I like to perform, especially baroque,

contrapuntal music, is that for a short period of time, I am fully in control. I enjoy knowing that when I push my fingers down in a certain, disciplined way, I will hear music that I love. Always. I am never disappointed.

But there are very few things I can control in the same way. I am still trying to accept that fact. Brigham Young University provost Bruce Hafen beautifully explains the boundaries of human control: "From God's perspective on our lives, we can control the things that really matter: the righteousness of our desires, the purity of our motives, the wholeheartedness of our efforts to love God and keep his commandments, the genuineness of our interest in other people, and the extent to which our efforts reflect our inborn capacity. One way to distinguish what matters a great deal from what does not matter so much is to ask whether the subject is within our control. If it is, then it probably matters enough to merit our attention. But if the object of our fretting is inherently beyond our control, God is unlikely to hold us responsible for our ultimate success or failure as to that concern."[2]

I do not mean to imply that I want to control other people's lives. I would, however, like to control my own. But even that is not really possible. My life has had many sharp turns with unexpected and unpredictable results. Some, like the one that brought me to the Tabernacle organ, have been good; others have been difficult and painful.

I am trying now to be less controlling of everyone, including myself, recognizing the importance of agency. I am trying to be more trusting in the Lord—trusting that he will move me where he wants me. Most of all, I am trying to increase my faith—faith in the Atonement and in the promise "that all things work together for good to them that love God" (Romans 8:28).

NOTES

1. See Arnold Scheibel, "You Can Continuously Improve Your Mind and Your Memory," *Bottom Line/Personal* 21 (1 November 1994): 9–10. Professor

Scheibel, director of the Brain Research Institute, University of California, has found that learning to play a musical instrument or taking your basic musical skill to a more advanced level stimulates mental function.

2.   Bruce Hafen, *The Broken Heart* (Salt Lake City: Deseret Book, 1989), 101–2.

MY GRANDMOTHER PAINTED

ELISA PULIDO

When my grandmother married, she left
New York, the art institute, and Henri
and went west, where she painted Brigham Young,
Jim Bridger, and Indians wrapped in magenta
blankets riding pinto mustangs through sage-
colored hills. She painted her husband
and cottonwoods and flowers from the funerals
of her friends, and Martha, and Mary kneeling
at Jesus' feet—all on an easel
in her living room, after scrubbing
bottles for the town dairy, before cooking
for ranch hands, while wash for five children
dried in the wind.

                    She studied her canvas
through a diminishing glass "for perspective,"
she said. Still the distance of hay fields
from the house was such that children
(dressed in green or red to be easily seen)
were sometimes lost. Then Grandma would toss
her brushes and run towards the ditch, promising
God, that if he would bring this one child home
she would never paint again.

Elisa Pulido graduated from Brigham Young University with a bachelor of arts degree in German and received a teaching credential from California State–San Bernardino. She also served a mission in the Switzerland Zurich mission. Elisa has three children and resides with her husband in Madrid, Spain, where she teaches seminary and serves on the stake public affairs committee.

THE THINNESS OBSESSION

HAROLD A. FROST

Anorexia, bulimia, compulsive eating—these are familiar words to most women today. One in a hundred females has anorexia nervosa, and almost 15 percent of female college students have bulimia.[1] Most of us, however, have no concept of the full emotional upheaval and medical complications these eating disorders cause. I first learned how to diagnose eating disorders in 1974 in an abnormal psychology class. At that time, my class was told that those of us who would be working clinically in the area of psychology would be unlikely to see more than one or two eating disorders patients in our whole career. The reality of the 1990s is that I see twenty to thirty patients a week, all of them with eating disorders.

What might lead you to suspect that you or someone you love has an eating disorder? An anorexic person goes to extreme measures to restrict calories and burn them off, eating perhaps only three hundred calories a day and running eight or nine miles in an effort to be thin. Anorexics also abuse laxatives, diuretics, enemas, and diet pills. Their intense fear of becoming obese and their eating habits eventually interrupt their normal menstrual cycle.

Anorexics have a distorted view of what they look like. No matter how much weight they lose, they see themselves as fat.

Harold A. Frost is a licensed psychologist in private practice and president of the Center for Change, a residential program for women suffering with eating disorders. Brother Frost resides with his wife, Sue Anne Frost, and their three children in Orem, Utah. He serves in the high priest group leadership in his ward.

Let me give you an example. Several years ago, a stake president from Garden Grove, California, sent a young woman to me for treatment. Pictures she brought of herself taken before her eating disorder showed that she had been very beautiful. In fact, she had won the Miss Garden Grove title, standing 5'8" and weighing 120 pounds—slender for her height. When we received her at the hospital, she was still 5'8" but weighed only 60 pounds. And yet one of the first things she did was grab a fold of skin on her stomach and say, "See, Dr. Frost? See how fat I am? If I could only weigh five pounds less then I could live happily ever after."

Bulimic women also want to be thin, but they go about it differently. A woman with bulimia will eat large quantities of food, usually secretly, in a short time—called a binge—and then purge in an attempt to rid herself of calories. The most typical type of purging is vomiting. I've had patients who force themselves to throw up as many as forty times a day. Other women use laxatives to purge. One of my patients was taking two hundred Ex-Lax a day. Her whole life was spent roaming from grocery store to grocery store, buying and stealing Ex-Lax and candy bars. Still other women purge by exercising obsessively or fasting after a binge. This bingeing and purging is often cyclic.

Many women suffer from both anorexia nervosa and bulimia. Less serious but perhaps more prevalent is compulsive eating, which is basically binge eating. Compulsive eaters, too, have a desire to be thin, but they cope with their life by constantly eating. The more they focus on not wanting to eat, the more they think about food. These compulsive thoughts eventually lead them to the kitchen cupboard.

Sooner or later, women with serious eating disorders will develop serious medical complications. Insomnia, constipation, dry skin, hair loss, weak and brittle nails, and feeling cold are danger signs. Sore throats, tooth decay, gum disease, and swelling of the cheeks are an inevitable consequence of constantly bathing your mouth and teeth in stomach acid. Some of my patients have lost all their teeth as a result of incessant purging. Dentists are starting to recognize the connection between purging and dental problems. Recently a dentist told me, "On our final exam in dental school we were shown a picture of a young woman whose teeth were eroded starting at the back and going to the front. 'What is wrong with this young woman's mouth?' the exam read." Of course, the correct answer is that she is struggling with bulimia nervosa.

Victims of serious eating disorders almost always suffer from malnutrition. Osteoporosis, or the thinning of bones, is another medical complication. One woman I saw at the hospital had, as a result of her incessant anorexia and bulimia, shrunk from 5'8" to 5'3". When she was in the hospital, she reached across her bed to get a book and cracked a rib! The heart is also affected by eating disorders. I work with a twenty-seven-year-old woman who has already had three heart attacks. The first patient I lost, in 1987, died of heart complications.

Science and statistics can, however, distance us from the real loss. Details from one person's story may capture the human problem. A patient of mine—I'll call her Francie—has kindly allowed me to share part of her life that she kept secret for a long time.

FRANCIE'S STORY

Hi. My name is Francie. I'm twenty-six years old, and I'm anorexic. I have been this way for years. I started gymnastics at the age of six, and I competed until I was thirteen when I switched to cheerleading. I was a cheerleader all through high school and for three years at college. I think that's where my issues with weight and food really started. We were weighed every day, and everybody knew how much you weighed and how much body fat you had. Since I was one of the tinier girls, I was a flyer, and it was even more important to be light. The lighter and skinnier you were, the better cheerleader you were. That's when I decided that being skinny meant being good enough. And so I started starving. I tried every diet there was. The cheerleaders taught each other dieting tricks: water pills, diet pills, starve yourself for six days and eat for one.

I come from a perfectionist family. In high school during my sophomore and junior years, I'd go to my father's office for help with writing a paper. By 11:30 or 12 at night, I would be on the couch falling asleep, saying, "I don't care what grade the teacher gives me. I just want to go home. I'm tired." I was sixteen. But my father would hold my paper up to the light, making sure that all the page numbers lined up on top of each other and that the first lines and the last lines of each paper lined up right on top of each other. "Just one more time," he'd say. "Let's print it out just one more time. Let's just change three words in this last paragraph. Just one more minute. It will just take a minute." I think that's where I learned to expect perfection from myself. I'm either number one or I have failed. There is no second place for me. There is no third place. There is no average.

My mother has struggled with food all of her life as well. When we went out to dinner, she never ordered her own meal. She only ate off my dad's plate. She didn't hit a hundred pounds until I was a senior in high school and by then I was a 105. I was giving her pants that I had grown out of. I think I learned my eating habits from her.

I run eight to ten miles every day. Remember, I'm a perfectionist. Everything is black or white for me. I decide every day when I get up in the morning how far I need to run that day and the time I need to do it in. If I run out of time and get off that treadmill even two minutes early, I have to go back to the gym. And not only do I have to make up for that quarter of a mile I missed, I have to run an extra two to make up for getting off early. Sometimes I go back to the gym two or three times in one day.

When I moved to Provo to attend Brigham Young University, I got involved in an emotionally abusive relationship. I dated a boy for about three and a half years, and every day for that three and a half years he told me I wasn't good enough. I wasn't funny enough. I wasn't sweet enough. I wasn't smart enough. I wasn't skinny enough. I wasn't . . . I went from thing to thing, trying to be perfect, trying to make him love me.

But no matter what I did, he kept saying, "If you'll just do this, then I'll love you." So I would do it. "No, that's not it. If you'll just do this, then I'll love you." It was such a roller coaster. When he got to not skinny enough, I had already had practice. I was really good at that. So I starved and I started exercising. Food and exercise were really the only things that I felt I *could* control. I needed control. And that control was all mine, something I knew I was really good at.

If you know or suspect someone close to you has an eating disorder, the best thing is to support them without trying to control their food. Don't police their food or follow them to the bathroom after they eat. The food is just the symptom; somewhere in their lives they feel out of control, if not everywhere. Just be there for them; find out what's really going on in their lives.

EATING DISORDERS ARE AN ADDICTION

Perhaps you sensed from Francie's remarks that eating disorders really are an addiction, and they are far more complex than they appear. In spite of the terrible consequences of eating disorders, I believe they are a way to manage pain. Let me illustrate with a letter I received from a sister missionary:

"Dear Dr. Frost,

"Hello, it's me. I just thought I'd drop you a line and tell you how things are going. To be honest with you, I have had culture shock in the worst way. This is the worst thing I have ever gone through. Being a missionary in SLC was like paradise compared to here. Every day I ask myself, 'Self, why are you doing this?' I get the same answer, 'I don't know.' All I wanted to do was serve the Lord and be good at it. The language has been a major barrier. I basically understand the people but as far as talking, I don't. It's just a lot easier to be silent than to try and make up conversation. I never was good at idle chat and now in Spanish, forget it!!!

"Ok, now to the stuff you want to know. Yes, I have thrown up. I guess I like talking to the toilet because there is nobody else to talk to. It wasn't even because I binged. I think it's because I feel I have lost control of everything. I float around here like a tumbleweed. . . .

"We have no scales so I'm always thinking I'm gaining weight. Now I don't want to eat anything because I think it goes right to my hips. . . . Sometimes I wonder if I'm using that as an escape. Maybe I think that getting rid of the food will get rid of my problems? Who knows? . . . I haven't done it more than once a day so it's still at the same point. I'll tell you if it gets worse. If you have any advice, please write. Thanks for listening."

I'm sorry to tell you that this young woman terminated her mission far short of completion.

It's easy for me to understand why the overwhelming majority of those with eating disorders are female. Women learn early and from diverse sources—their family, television, movies, the fashion industry—the message that appearance is of supreme importance: the body is where their value lies. Ambrose Bierce, a nineteenth-century satirist, summed it up: "To men a man is but a mind. Who cares what face he carries? Or what form he wears? But a woman's body is the woman."[2] When I read this quotation to Relief Society women, they nod their heads knowingly. Only a hundred years ago, women were told that if they overstimulated their brains by going to college, their ovaries would atrophy. We must be careful what we buy into. Pushing ourselves to be perfect, when perfection is impossible, often causes families to place undue importance on externals—appearance and achievement, being first and best.

Carol Lynn Pearson offers some good advice in *Blow Out the Wishbone:* "This morning I was hugging and kissing Katy (my fourth child), and I said to her, 'Oh, Katy—how did I get you? I must have won the contest and you were first prize!'

"Katy laughed. 'Oh, no, Mom. I was fourth prize!'

"Fourth prize? *You?* Absurd!

"Do you know what, Katy? We human beings have got ourselves into such trouble since we learned how to count. Does there always have to be a first and a last, a best and a worst, or even a better than?

"Is first best? You put on your socks first and your shoes second. Does that mean your socks are better than your shoes? The Bible says that Adam was created first and Eve second, and lots of people think that makes man better than woman. But the horse was made before Adam. Does that make the horse better than man? You see, it gets very tricky. We have made up our games with our numbers and our prizes and we give out our ribbons and sometimes it helps and sometimes it messes us up.

"Go ahead and do your math papers, my dear. But sometimes let's forget we ever learned how to count. We're not numbered. We just *are.* And you know what we're going to find out one day? We're all *first prize!*"[3]

People with eating disorders have hopes and dreams, just like everybody else; they seek love, success, happiness, and acceptance. But they have been misguided in their efforts to find these things. They have been led to believe that they must always win "first prize." When they fall short of perfection in any area, they feel like failures. From my patients, I hear:

I am defective/damaged/broken/a mistake/flawed.

I am incompetent/not good enough/ineffectual/useless.

I deserve criticism/condemnation/disapproval/destruction.

These kinds of feelings stunt emotional and spiritual growth. Spiritual healing is the real key to healing eating disorders. With the right kind of help, love, and encouragement, and with patience—people with eating disorders can return to a knowledge of "things as they really are" (see Jacob 4:13). We need to see ourselves as God sees us—as important, lovable, cherished children, whatever our current imperfections. One of my patients, in despair took every medicine in her medicine cabinet. She was in a coma for three weeks. While the doctors were telling her parents that she probably would not pull through, her only memory was the Lord sitting at her bedside telling her she would. A scale can only tell you how much you weigh. It can't even begin to tell you how much you matter to God.

NOTES

1. Susan C. Wooley and Ann Kearney-Cooke, "Intensive Treatment of Bulimia and Body-Image Disturbance," in Kelly D. Brownell and John P. Foreyt, eds., *Handbook of Eating Disorders* (New York City: Basic Books, 1986), 477.

2. Ambrose Bierce, *The Devil's Dictionary* (New York City: Dover Press, 1958).

3. Carol Lynn Pearson, *Blow Out the Wishbone* (Salt Lake City: Bookcraft, 1985), 20–21.

SPIRITUAL BELIEFS AND EATING DISORDERS

LYNNE A. BENNION

Mary is an attractive young college student who stands 5'5" and weighs 140 pounds. She is very bright and is doing well in school. Mary constantly compares her body to those of other women around her, nearly always concluding that she is uglier and fatter than they are and that no man will ever be interested in her. Mary has a great secret that she tries to hide from everyone: she is bulimic. She binge eats when she is feeling stressed or depressed. During a typical binge, she may eat an entire box of sweetened cereal, three candy bars, a bag of tortilla chips, and a large bowl of ice cream. She then makes herself vomit and afterwards feels disgusted with herself for being so "weak and out of control." If Mary continues this pattern of bulimia, she will experience medical complications, including excessive dental cavities and damage to her esophagus and digestive tract.

This profile of a bulimic woman is based on the symptoms of several real-life clients that I have seen during the past nine years in my practice as a clinical psychologist. In addition to clients with very chaotic or very restricted eating patterns, I have seen others with somewhat healthier eating habits who

Lynne A. Bennion has a Ph.D. in clinical psychology and is an assistant clinical professor in counseling and development at Brigham Young University. She is a member of her ward's employment committee.

have experienced a great deal of distress about the way their bodies look.

Research has shown that the causes of eating disorders are often complex. One factor can be the individual's typical pattern of thinking about herself and her world: beliefs and attitudes can make us either more or less vulnerable to struggles with self-esteem and body image. I have observed that religious beliefs can strongly affect how we view and treat our bodies. I will discuss four religious beliefs common to my clients with eating disorders.

The first belief is deeply rooted in our cultural history: *One of the best ways to show devotion to God is to suffer. Pleasure is bad;*[1] *suffering is virtuous. We must overcome all pleasure.*[2]

The Greek philosopher Plato believed that the spiritual and material worlds were separate realms and that the material world was inferior to the realm of ideals. In his view, the body drags the spirit downward, so one should escape the limitations of the body by fasting or denying oneself in other ways. In the Christian church, fasting did not become an extensive community practice until about the third century after Christ. During the third or fourth centuries, some Christians became increasingly intent on denying themselves any pleasure and purposely inflicting pain on themselves: for example, they starved themselves to root out the pleasure of eating, deprived themselves of sleep, and whipped their bodies in an attempt to force the body toward virtue.

In medieval Europe, several women (some of whom became Christian saints) had similarly extreme ideas. For example, one woman subsisted on only a few herbs or seeds: she would put five seeds into her mouth, suck on them, and spit them out. These women inflicted pain and suffering on themselves in various other ways as well. Their reasons for fasting obsessively (to the point where some died of starvation) are complex; however, one motive seems to have been the belief that denying themselves food proved holiness.

221

Thus, at various times in the history of the world certain people have believed that one of the best ways to show devotion to God is to suffer—not just experience the natural suffering that comes from living on a planet with natural laws and human agency but to seek purposely to deny themselves pleasure and inflict pain on themselves.

Several scriptures suggest that, on the contrary, God's intention is for us to experience joy and life: "For I have no pleasure in the death of him that dieth, saith the Lord God: wherefore turn yourselves, and live ye" (Ezekiel 18:32). "Adam fell that men might be; and men are, that they might have joy" (2 Nephi 2:25).

Isaiah addressed those who fast by "afflicting" themselves, suggesting that the Lord hopes we will experience a different kind of fast: "Wherefore have we fasted, say they, and thou seest not? wherefore have we afflicted our soul, and thou takest no knowledge? . . . is it such a fast that I have chosen? a day for man to afflict his soul? is it to bow down his head as a bulrush, and to spread sackcloth and ashes under him? wilt thou call this a fast, and an acceptable day to the Lord? Is not this the fast that I have chosen? to loose the bands of wickedness, to undo the heavy burdens, and to let the oppressed go free, and that ye break every yoke? Is it not to deal thy bread to the hungry, and that thou bring the poor that are cast out to thy house? when thou seest the naked, that thou cover him; and that thou hide not thyself from thine own flesh? Then shall thy light break forth as the morning, and thine health shall spring forth speedily" (58:3–8). The Savior declared, "I am come that they might have life, and that they might have it more abundantly" (John 10:10).

These scriptures suggest to me that in choosing mortality under conditions of natural law and human agency, we do suffer, but suffering, or proving that we are holy by suffering, is not the main point. I want to keep the Lord's commandments not to be good but because in doing the things that God has recommended as good I will find joy and life.

The Word of Wisdom suggests the importance of nurturing and caring for our bodies so that we can be healthy, think clearly, and have energy. Although this health code details some specifics, such as the point that tobacco is "not good for man," many others are not mentioned (D&C 89:8). For example, the list does not include, "Don't put your tongue on the inside of a freezer. Don't cross the street in dark clothes at night without looking both ways." While we tend to emphasize all the things we should not do, the Word of Wisdom suggests that it is just as important to think about all the things we can do to take good care of our bodies. The Word of Wisdom teaches us that our bodies are important, our bodies are good, and our bodies are worth caring for.

In sum, to counter the belief that it is virtuous to suffer, I propose that God wants us to find joy, and he hopes we will nourish and take care of our bodies.

A second religious belief that prevails among some persons with eating disorders, *A righteous person does not get angry or sad. I must therefore control and conquer all of my urges and all of my feelings.*

Many persons who struggle with eating disorders find it very difficult to identify, acknowledge, accept, and appropriately express feelings. These individuals often come from families that discouraged or even punished expression of certain feelings. In some families that was done overtly; in others it was communicated in subtle, indirect ways.

An important part of managing eating habits is discovering one's own high-risk situations. For example, during what emotional states might you feel an urge to binge eat? For some women, it is when they feel angry. For others, it may be when they feel lonely, bored, or overwhelmed. A next step is to identify and then use other ways to soothe these feelings. The goal

223

is not simply to stop the pleasure or comfort of eating but to substitute other appropriate comforts or pleasures.

I had a bulimic client who binged nearly every day, usually when she got home from school. During our initial interview, she stated that everything else in her life was under control: if she could just stop bingeing, everything would be perfect. All her efforts to solve the bingeing had involved controlling her life more tightly. As we talked, we discovered that the binges were the *only* time during the day when she was not in complete control—the only time when she allowed herself to experience pleasure; the only time when she allowed herself to be spontaneous. Paradoxically, as therapy progressed, she found that in letting go of controlling every last thing, scheduling time to "tune in" to what she was feeling and allowing herself little chunks of time to unwind, her bingeing episodes significantly decreased. Though recovery from an eating disorder usually takes time and a long-term commitment, improving awareness and appropriate expression of feelings is often a critical early step.

According to traditional psychodynamic theory, the notion that we can absolutely control feelings is something of a myth anyway: unexpressed feelings tend to stockpile. From this theoretical perspective, depression is defined as "anger turned inward." I believe that emotions are helpful tools. When we ignore them, we ignore problems that need attention. For example, a young married couple bought a home that had not been well maintained by its previous owner. The husband, Tim, began fixing things: he installed wiring for a dryer in the basement, repaired and painted a broken storm door, and so on. Tim thought he was being a good husband by taking care of his wife. Ellen, his wife, whose father had taught her how to use tools, had been looking forward to working with Tim on the house repairs. When Tim took control of projects and did not ask for her opinions or assistance, Ellen felt angry but "politely" decided not to say anything about it. Instead she went into the kitchen and ate a whole batch of cookie dough. In the following week, Tim noticed that Ellen seemed quiet, withdrawn, and occasionally critical of little things he did. Tim felt anxious, interpreting her changed behavior as a sign that she did not love him as much anymore, but he did not want to "make things worse" by talking about it. By ignoring their emotional cues of anger and anxiety and by attempting to avoid conflict, Tim and Ellen missed the opportunity to learn important information about each other.

Distinguishing between an emotion and the way one chooses to express it is important. To acknowledge feelings of anger places a person in a position to choose from a variety of ways to express the anger.

In sum, to counter the beliefs that we should never be sad or angry, I suggest that these feelings are important tools that can help us solve problems that would otherwise prevent close relationships with others. I believe God wants us to be feeling persons rather than sterile, unemotional beings. He cares about the emotions we feel. I believe God wants us to pray to him, even when we are angry or sad, without feeling shame for having those feelings. His main interest is to help and comfort us rather than judge us.

A third religious belief that I have observed in the thinking of many clients with eating disorders is, *If I do the right things, all will go well for me. If things are not going well, it's my fault—I must be doing something wrong.* It can be scary to live in a world in which we cannot control everything that happens to us; no one likes to feel helpless. The reality for all of us, whether or not we are working hard to live good lives, is that we experience both control *and* lack of it, both pleasure *and* pain. As Christ noted in the Sermon on the Mount, "Your Father which is in heaven . . . maketh his sun to rise on the evil and on the good, and sendeth rain on the just and on the unjust" (Matthew 5:45).

Among the many theories proposed to explain human

suffering, my opinion is that we asked to come to a world where we could experience good and evil, pain and pleasure, natural laws, and agency—both ours and others'—because we saw value in learning how to deal with reality. If we live in certain ways, we are less likely to experience certain problems, but we cannot control everything. I believe that if we ask the Lord for help, he will help us eventually get through problems that arise because of natural laws or human agency. Carrying *unrealistic* guilt—guilt for things over which we have little or no control, or guilt for being less than perfect at all times—is unnecessary and can impede our progress.

A fourth confusion for some persons with eating disorders arises when they transfer to God attributes from their experiences with human beings: *Boys don't like fat girls. Being fat is bad and weak. Men like my father or the boys I went to high school with don't like fat girls. God probably doesn't like me as much if I'm overweight. If I'm skinny, other people and God will love me more.*

Freud and other theorists have believed that people develop an image of God—their idea of what he is like—based at least in part on their experiences with parents and other people they know. Nevertheless, I would argue that our experiences with God—as we pray, for example—can also influence our sense of what he is like, though I agree that our experiences with human beings may influence how we perceive God and whether we feel unsafe approaching him to find out how he actually feels about us.

One such human experience can be the pressure to be "in style." Being in style not only places emphasis on outward appearance rather than the heart but also involves a status differential, or hierarchy: for you to be in style, someone else has to be out of style. According to this human philosophy, a woman must not only be beautiful and slender to be valuable but *more* beautiful and *more* slender than other women.

In the world of fashion, many companies actively promote

this status differential to make money. A clothing company is not going to make much money designing and selling a new line of products if people feel they look fine in the clothes hanging in their closets. If an advertisement can make you believe that people will like you better if you are skinny, wear their clothes, or use their make-up, you may feel uncomfortable enough to spend money to look "better."

Having been taught by the media and others with earthly viewpoints that their value lies in their appearance, many women believe that others will like them better when they are skinny. A few of my clients have lost a hundred or more pounds and found, to their great disappointment, that they did not suddenly have more dates or more friends. Other clients note that people do seem more responsive to them when they weigh less. With further discussion, however, these clients come to realize that when they feel better about themselves (because of weight loss or any other reason), they are more open and warm. Others naturally respond to them with more friendliness. It is primarily their openness, rather than their body weight, that seems to make them more attractive.

Similarly, I have had clients who, when praying, approached the Lord with heavy shame, believing that their Father in Heaven was disappointed in them for one reason or another. Sometimes they had in mind a specific reason why God should dislike or be angry with them: for example, because they had not "controlled" their diet that day, or because they had not prayed for some time. Sometimes they had no specific weakness in mind but felt they were simply worthless in general. Just as people close themselves to others' friendliness when they feel ashamed and thus cannot detect the warmth that others actually feel for them, so humans may approach the Lord with so much conviction that they are no good that they are not open to receiving the warmth that he does indeed feel for them. My understanding of God is that he invites us to come to him at all times.

Several scriptures indicate that God does not share earthly notions of what makes us valuable. For instance, it is written in 1 Samuel 16:7 that "the Lord seeth not as man seeth; for man looketh on the outward appearance, but the Lord looketh on the heart." A similar statement is found in Isaiah: "My thoughts are not your thoughts, neither are your ways my ways" (55:8). My own experience has been that God's love for me does not depend on my physical appearance or on my performance: he already loves me and values me. How I compare to others around me does not change God's feelings for me. Moreover, eternal progression involves never-ending opportunities for change and growth. In mortal life people are indeed dealt unequal hands, but over time we will all be given opportunities to overcome all obstacles and limitations.

To summarize, the scriptures and my experience with God suggest that God's interest is to help us, comfort us, and save us. He wants us to be happy. He knows we will also experience sorrow, anger, loneliness, frustration, and many other human emotions. In the process, he invites us to nourish and care for both our bodies and our souls.

When Laman and Lemuel were complaining that they could not understand all the things their father had been telling them about the Lord, Nephi asked them, "Have ye inquired of the Lord?" (1 Nephi 15:8). It can be scary to ask God directly to help you understand your own value or to help you feel his love for you. But it seems that we may learn how to love only *after* we have experience with being loved: "Beloved, let us love one another: for love is of God; and everyone that loveth is born of God, and knoweth God. He that loveth not knoweth not God; for God is love. . . . There is no fear in love; but perfect love casteth out fear: because fear hath torment. He that feareth is not made perfect in love. We love him, because he first loved us" (1 John 4:7–8, 18–19).

Mormon also invites us to inquire of the Lord: "Pray unto the Father with all the energy of heart, that ye may be filled with his love [the pure of Christ]" (Moroni 7:48). I believe that Mormon's words are not just an admonition to ask for love so you can love others but also an invitation to ask to feel God's love for you. We can seek the Lord's help in understanding our worth and how to love ourselves and each other appropriately. When we feel God's love, everything becomes different, including how we view and take care of our bodies.

Recovering from a well-entrenched eating disorder is usually a long and difficult process. Some people experiment only briefly with severely restricted diets and/or vomiting as weight-loss strategies, but those who continue those behaviors over time usually do so for reasons other than or in addition to simple weight regulation (for example, to sooth intense feelings). I believe that medical consultation, individual and group psychotherapy, and other forms of professional treatment can be helpful to these people. Identifying and revising spiritual beliefs and seeking help from the Lord to understand their own individual worth can also be an important part of recovery.

NOTES

1. People who are most at risk for eating disorders, depression, and low self-esteem generally label behavior and themselves as either bad or good. For them, bad/good is a global, dichotomous construct that can subsume almost everything. *Bad* is the word I've heard most of my clients with eating disorders use to describe themselves. It is a word they first hear used as a little child, and for some people whose cognitive/emotional development was slowed or arrested early in life (through trauma, lack of parental responsiveness to emotional expression, or a number of other possible circumstances), moral reasoning is better characterized by "good/bad" (good-me, bad-me) than the more narrow term "sinful."

2. For an ascetic with an eating disorder, it can be difficult to distinguish between desire and the expression of desire, or to distinguish between desire and the experience of feeling pleasure. The thought patterns of such persons tend to be dichotomus and global. Also, the boundaries between "self" and "body" often become blurred.

BREAST CANCER: ONE IN NINE

SAUNDRA BUYS

Breast cancer affects many women in this country, and it affects Latter-day Saint women at about the same rate as everyone else. What is that rate? A lot of women carry around the "one in nine" figure. Does this mean that if you and eight friends all get a mammogram the same day, one of you will end up being diagnosed with breast cancer? No. It means that if a woman is born today and lives to age eighty-five, she has a one in nine chance of getting breast cancer sometime in those eighty-five years. Another way to think about the likelihood of breast cancer is to consider: what's my chance of getting breast cancer in the next ten years? For a forty-year-old, that likelihood is between 1 and 2 percent. So one in nine is accurate in some sense, and breast cancer is common, but it is not as frighteningly common as a lot of people think.

As an oncologist, I would like to discuss some facts about breast cancer—basic concepts that women who get breast cancer should understand to make good decisions about dealing with it. Second, I'd like to stress that early detection of breast cancer is important in achieving the highest likelihood of cure. Finally, I will include some practical advice for women who have breast cancer and for the people who care about them.

Cancer is out-of-control cell growth. Normal cells line up

Saundra Buys is an associate professor in the Division of Hematology/Oncology at the University of Utah School of Medicine. She is also director of the High-Risk Breast Cancer Clinic at the Huntsman Cancer Institute. She has served as ward choir director and Gospel Doctrine teacher. Saundra and her husband, Joe, have two children.

230

nicely in a row; cancerous cells accumulate and pile up. Instead of being inhibited by their neighbors on either side, cancerous cells just keep on growing. In time, they invade surrounding tissue. From there they can spread elsewhere in the body. You would not find a normal breast cell in the bone, for example, but a cancerous breast cell could be found in the bone. These two characteristics of cancer—the ability to invade into surrounding tissue and the ability to spread elsewhere in the body—are important principles that guide how we think about treating the disease.

Cancer is caused both by genetic factors (genes) that we get from parents, and nongenetic or environmental factors, such as our age, diet, whether or not we have children and at what age we start having them, how much estrogen we have in our bodies, and maybe such things as how much we exercise and where we live. Notice that nothing in either genetic or nongenetic causes of cancer suggests we get cancer because we deserve it. Some people want so much to believe they can control what happens to them that they would almost rather believe that they did something to deserve it than to face the fact that life sometimes isn't fair.

Breast cancer is more likely to be cured if it is detected early, before it has spread. It can be found in three ways: breast self-examination, clinical examination by a doctor or nurse, and mammogram. Mammograms are an effective tool for detecting breast cancer, though most cancers are detected by women themselves. It's recommended that women examine their breasts every month starting at age twenty.

Normal breast tissue has some texture to it, and that confuses a lot of women. They say, "I don't know what I'm feeling. I always feel lumpy." I've heard women describe their breast tissue as having a Rice Krispies kind of feeling. What they are describing is normal fat and breast glands, and that's okay. Some women have cysts that are round and smooth and easily movable. Having fibrocystic breasts, as these are called,

231

doesn't increase your risk of breast cancer. They just make it harder to detect, because cysts and cancer can be hard to tell apart on exam. If you are doing good breast self-exams and know what your breasts feel like, then the cancers you may detect are more likely to be small than large.

Let me offer some practical advice. First, if you find a breast lump, don't dillydally for months and months about getting a diagnosis. If somebody tells you not to worry about the lump and you are worried about it, don't stay quiet. Speak up. Go back to your doctor. If that doctor doesn't want to do anything, go to another doctor. If you've got a lump, then it needs to be evaluated. On the other hand, if you have been diagnosed with breast cancer, you don't need to feel like you have to do something *this second*. You've got time to think about it, to talk to people, to get second opinions. It's all right to take a few days or a week or two.

Good information is very important. The National Cancer Institute and the American Cancer Society offer many helpful books and brochures. In the rush to get information, though, be careful who you listen to. Take what you hear with a grain of salt. When I was first pregnant, I was shocked at how many people wanted to tell me horror stories about their pregnancies, their deliveries, and their first child. I was surprised to find that the whole experience was not really bad at all. And a lot of people—I used to call them well-meaning, but I'm not sure they are—will want to tell you gruesome stories about their next-door neighbor's experience with cancer. So be cautious about who you listen to, particularly if these voices are suggesting that you are in any way to blame for what's happening to you.

Support groups can be very useful. Not all women need them, but most gain a lot from them. I've heard women say, "It was such a relief to hear someone else express my fears and my anger and my anxiety." Sometimes you don't want to say things to your family for fear of worrying them, but your support group is happy to hear you complain about your doctor or your husband, or worry about your kids.

Finally, like any other big, life-changing experience—having a child, or having someone die—breast cancer is not something you get over in three months or six months or a year. The experience stays with you. As one very honest patient joked on a follow-up visit, "Oh, I'm just fine—except for my twenty recurrences a day." Every little symptom, sign, or suspicion may be much more frightening once you've had breast cancer. As with any other significant experience, then, breast cancer permanently changes people. In my experience, this change is for the better. Women often emerge from the breast cancer experience stronger, more confident of their ability to face and overcome challenges, more secure in important relationships, more empathetic, and more clear on their priorities.

FEAR NOT

AILEEN H. CLYDE

It's quite wonderful when your breast cancer surgery was so long ago that you have to stop and think about how long it has been. I am more grateful as each year passes to put one more year between that time of fear and the present.

I was diagnosed with breast cancer in 1987, as were two other women in my ward. All three of us were afraid, yet we dealt with that fear in different ways. Our ages, too, were different. I was by far the oldest, being in my sixty-first year; the youngest had just passed her forty-first birthday. She had detected a lump in her breast a year before but because of her age had chosen to assume it was nothing. She pushed thoughts of any danger from her mind. (When we get fearful, we don't think much—we feel things, but we don't think much.) Time passed, and she could still feel the lump. It did not go away. She later told us she had felt that by not talking to anyone about the lump, she was somehow containing it and her fears.

After nearly a year, she arranged for a screening in another city. That, too, was irrationally motivated. She was now ready to peek at what the reality might be, but by going to a place where she was not known, she thought she could somehow continue to control consequences by controlling her privacy. The medical examination confirmed that her condition needed

Aileen H. Clyde has served as second counselor in the General Relief Society presidency. She and her husband, Hal M. Clyde, are the parents of three married sons. She has also served as vice chairman of the board of regents of the Utah System of Higher Education. She graduated from Brigham Young University and was an English instructor there.

234

immediate attention. She was advised to go to a surgeon immediately for further diagnosis and treatment. When she finally did that, months after the screening, tests proved that the cancer had metastasized, or spread, and her prognosis was very grave.

My story was quite different. A full twenty years before 1987, I had awakened one morning, just a week before our first son was to leave for his mission, feeling excited and energetic. I had many things lined up to do that week. As I showered that morning, I noticed a lump in my breast. It was a shock, but my first impulse was to ask someone what should be done next. I immediately called my brother, a physician. "Well, don't dillydally about this. Go to someone immediately and have it diagnosed," he said. I did. He referred me to a surgeon who examined me and thought the lump should be biopsied. I sat in his office, nervously listening, as he canceled an early surgery the next day and scheduled mine instead.

I called my husband to tell him of the change of plans, and he and our soon-to-be missionary son came to accompany me to the hospital. The doctor had explained that if a frozen section of the biopsy indicated a malignant tumor, I should prepare to awaken from the anesthetic having had a mastectomy. All of this was disconcerting, but the step-by-step action seemed necessary and sensible. The crisis passed quickly when the biopsy showed the lump to be a benign cyst. When I had several other cysts at later times, I was happy to be treated by Dr. Charles Smart who aspirated them by removing fluid from the cyst with a needle. This procedure caused the cysts to collapse, eliminating the need for general anesthetic and surgery. Dr. Smart, who still is engaged in a lot of breast cancer research, said, "Cystic breast disease is not a serious matter at all unless you wake up one day and find a lump and think, Oh I've had a dozen of these, and don't follow it through."

And so in 1987 when I found another very small lump, even though I could just barely feel it, I went to Dr. James McGreevy, the surgeon who had been recommended for my regular checkups by our youngest son when he was a medical student. (Dr. Smart had gone on to do research at the National Cancer Institute.) Dr. McGreevy could not detect the lump but suggested I have a mammogram a little ahead of my regularly scheduled one. The little lump, or whatever it was I was feeling, did not show up on the mammogram. "Well, let's wait a day or two," the doctor said. I went home, but I could still feel it. After a week I went back, and this time the doctor could feel it, too. He tried unsuccessfully to aspirate the lump, so the next step was a biopsy. When I went in for the procedure, the doctor said, "I'm sorry to put you through this. I'm 99 percent sure it's nothing." After the biopsy, he came out and said, "I was 99 percent wrong." Because the tumor was very small and seemed self-contained, I had a mastectomy. That made it unnecessary to have chemotherapy or follow-up radiation. I could have had a lumpectomy, but that option would have required six weeks of follow-up radiation. I had a busy time ahead of me and made my choice on that basis. Dr. McGreevy required me to consult with at least one other surgeon and a radiologist before making any decision. The biopsy was on Friday and by the following Monday, the mastectomy was done.

I offer this background information to show that I had kept track of my own health to the best of my ability over a period of time. I feel it is my responsibility to take care of my health. It didn't take a lot of time. I did breast self-examination routinely. I wasn't overly worried about cancer or preoccupied with lumps. But when I felt a lump, my experience told me to get professional help. When the mammogram did not show the lump I had felt and the doctor couldn't feel it, yet at home I could feel it again, I followed up on my perceptions. I think the persistent follow-through is important.

My other ward friend, the third woman, was in her middle fifties. She discovered her cancer on a routine physical examination just prior to a mission. She wasn't able to detect any lump, but her cancer showed on a routine mammogram. She elected to have a lumpectomy, which meant the removal of a portion of the breast surrounding the tumor. This procedure is always followed by radiation treatment and is now known to be statistically as satisfactory a cure as the more disfiguring mastectomy.

She, too, had immediate support from her family and sought clearly stated options, so she could make an informed decision about combating her cancer. Her mission service was delayed a few months by her treatment, but her good health since has caused her to comment often how grateful she is that a complete physical examination made early detection possible.

Both she and I remember with regret our dear sister, whom we loved, who has now passed away. With extensive treatment, our younger friend did live for three more years, but her cancer had progressed too far to be cured. She said to me many, many times during her illness, "If only I had said something to someone as you did, and we could have talked about it together." Once I knew about her cancer, I often went along with her for her treatments just to be with her. She found that consoling. At the beginning, there was something almost primordial about her fear of admitting to herself or to anyone else that she might have cancer. I learned from her experience that we need to be able to talk together about this frightening topic. Turning to one another with our fears may supply the support and encouragement some of us need to take appropriate action.

As I considered how often fear can interrupt or interfere with what we ought to do for ourselves or for others, I recalled the many times in scriptures we are counseled to be wise and to get understanding. One of my favorites is in Proverbs 3 beginning with verse 13: "Happy is the [woman] that findeth wisdom, and the [woman] that getteth understanding." That extends to all kinds of understanding. We are quite able to help one another work through whatever impediments there may be to accepting responsibility for our own health, however frightening that may sometimes seem to be.

INDEX